# EVERYDAY PRAYERS FOR GOD'S PEOPLE

C14円

Owen O'Sullivan OFM Cap

# Everyday Prayers
# for God's People

the columba press

First published in 2003 by
the columba press
55A Spruce Avenue, Stillorgan Industrial Park,
Blackrock, Co Dublin


Cover by Bill Bolger
Origination by The Columba Press
Printed in Ireland by ColourBooks Ltd, Dublin

ISBN 1 85607 372 6

Copyright acknowledgements are on page 122.

# Contents

Preface                                         7

Week 1                                         10
Week 2                                         38
Week 3                                         66
Week 4                                         94
References and Acknowledgements               122
Index of Authors, Sources and Terms           125
Index of Vatican II Documents                 151
Index of Psalms                               152
Index of Biblical Canticles                   153
Common Prayers                                154

# Preface

This book is written for beginners as well as for those who have been trying to pray for a long time. In the school of prayer we are all beginners. All of us feel the need, from time to time, for help with prayer. We are not always in top form, nor indeed do we need to be in order to pray. But we do need some help.

This is where the experience of the community of believers, stretching back to the writers of the Psalms who lived some 2,500 years ago, can come to our aid. This book offers their insights, as well as those of the Celtic tradition which draws on the natural world as a sign of God's abiding presence. The traditions of various Christian churches – Catholic, Anglican, Protestant and Orthodox – are drawn on. Between them they offer the reader comfort, challenge, encouragement and, perhaps, a fresh way of looking at God and the things of God.

The book can be used individually or in groups. In the latter case, preparation and maybe some adaptation are required.

A reader should not feel pressed to complete a section in one session. The best kind of prayer is that in which there is most love. And silence, a gentle listening silence may be closer to the heart of prayer than anything that is said. What matters is not to 'get through' the prayers but to give them quality time.

When we have made our best effort, we will still be conscious, sometimes painfully so, of our inadequacy. But that does not matter, because 'The Spirit helps us in our weakness; for we do not know how to pray as we ought, but that very Spirit intercedes for us with sighs too deep for words. And God, who searches the heart, knows what is the mind of the Spirit, because the Spirit intercedes for the saints according to the will of God.' (Romans 8:26-27)

Learning how to pray is like learning how to swim. You cannot escape the challenge of getting into the water and making an effort. No book will ever substitute for personal effort. This book will have served its purpose if it helps the reader to take the plunge and venture into prayer, which is a communion with God in the silence of the heart.

May the Lord bless you and keep you.

May he make his face to shine upon you, and be gracious to you.

May the Lord lift up his countenance upon you, and give you his peace.

(*Blessing of Saint Francis of Assisi, based on Numbers 6:24-26*)

*Everyday Prayers*

**Everything we do**

Lord, may everything we do begin with your inspiration and continue with your help, so that all our prayers and works may begin in you, and by you be happily ended; through Christ our Lord. Amen.

*(Adapted from the Roman liturgy)*

**Jesus Christ, the firstborn of all creation**

Let us give thanks to the Father who has enabled us to share in the inheritance of the saints in light.

He has delivered us from the power of darkness and transferred us into the Kingdom of his beloved Son, in whom we have redemption, the forgiveness of sins.

He is the image of the invisible God, the firstborn of all creation, for in him all things in heaven and on earth were created, things visible and invisible …

All things have been created through him and for him. He himself is before all things, and in him all things hold together. He is the head of the body, the church; he is the beginning, the firstborn from the dead, so that he might come to have first place in everything.

For in him all the fullness of God was pleased to dwell, and through him God was pleased to reconcile to himself all things, whether on earth or in heaven, by making peace through the blood of his cross.

*(Adapted from Colossians 1:12-20)*

**The sacrament of your Son**

Almighty God, I approach the sacrament of your Son, Jesus Christ. I come sick to the healer of life, sinful to the source of mercy, blind to eternal light, and poor to the Lord of heaven. In your goodness, heal my sickness, wash away my sins, enlighten my blindness, enrich my poverty, and cover my nakedness. May I receive the bread of angels with the humble reverence, the purity and faith, the repentance and love, and the determined purpose that will save me. May I receive the sacrament of the Lord's body and blood, really and truly. Kind God, may I receive the body and blood of your Son, Jesus Christ, born of the Virgin Mary, and be received into his body and counted among his members. Father, just as in this life I receive your Son in sacramental form, may I one day see him face to face in glory, he who lives with you for ever. Amen.

*(Saint Thomas Aquinas)*

**Prayer for a wife or husband**
Lord, so that I may come nearer to her (him), draw me nearer to you than to her (him). So that I may know her (him), make me know you more than her (him). So that I may love her (him) with the perfect love of a perfectly whole heart, cause me to love you more than her (him) and most of all. Amen.

*(Temple Gairdner)*

\* \* \*

*Reflections*

I received from the Lord what I also handed on to you, that the Lord Jesus, on the night when he was betrayed, took a loaf of bread, and when he had given thanks, he broke it and said, 'This is my body that is for you. Do this in remembrance of me.' In the same way he took the cup also, after supper, saying, 'This cup is the new covenant in my blood. Do this, as often as you drink it, in remembrance of me.' For as often as you eat this bread and drink the cup, you proclaim the Lord's death until he comes.

*(1 Corinthians 11:23-26)*

At this sacred banquet in which Christ is revealed, the memory of his passion is renewed, our lives are filled with grace, and a promise of future glory is given to us.

*(Saint Thomas Aquinas)*

Communion with God takes us out of ourselves and pushes us to alleviate human suffering in the world.

*(Mother Teresa of Calcutta)*

**Praise to the Trinity**

Be praised a thousand times, Father and Lamb; great and loving glory a thousand times over to the Son of God of victories; a thousand times honour, glory and praise to the surpassing fruit of creation, the Father, the Son and the Holy Spirit, until the day of judgment. Amen.

*(Celtic)*

**I believe in God**

I believe in God, the Father almighty, creator of heaven and earth.

I believe in Jesus Christ, his only Son, our Lord. He was conceived by the power of the Holy Spirit and born of the virgin Mary. He suffered under Pontius Pilate, was crucified, died, and was buried. He descended to the dead. On the third day he rose again. He ascended into heaven, and is seated at the right hand of God the Father. He will come again to judge the living and the dead.

I believe in the Holy Spirit, the holy catholic church, the communion of saints, the forgiveness of sins, the resurrection of the body, and the life everlasting. Amen.

*(Apostles' Creed)*

**Accept our thanksgiving**

Accept our thanksgiving, Lord God, you who are the fountain of all good, who have led us safely through this day, who daily bless us with so many mercies, and give us the hope of resurrection to eternal life; through Christ our Lord. Amen.

*(From an ancient collect)*

**For your church**

Lord, we thank you for your church throughout the world. Through your Holy Spirit, grant it life, strength and truth. Put into our hearts a constant love for it, and fill us with longing for the coming of your kingdom; through Christ our Lord. Amen.

*(Adapted from Pope Paul VI)*

**You are the light in my heart**

Lord, you are my refuge from the torment of the sins with which my heart besieges me. My joy is in you. Redeem me from the sorrow that my sins cause me. Because of my sins I am in darkness; but you, my God, will illuminate it. You are the truth and the light of my heart. Let me listen to you and not to the darkness within me. Lord, you are the light in my heart and the bread in the mouth of my soul.

Come, Lord, and act. Rouse and renew me; kindle me and carry me; shine before me and be gentle with me. Let me love and run towards you.

I pray to you, God, for you lead me to every truth, you tell me of every good thing, and you let me come to no harm. Amen.

*(Adapted from Saint Augustine)*

**Blessing**

May the Lord of peace himself give us peace at all times in all ways. The Lord be with all of us.

*(Adapted from 2 Thessalonians 3:16)*

\* \* \*

*Reflections*

If I tell the truth, why do you not believe in me?

*(John 8:46)*

Praised be God who has given us a mind that cannot be satisfied with the temporal.

*(Nicholas of Cusa)*

Let us do ever so little for God, we may be sure he will never forget it, nor let it pass unheeded.

*(Blessed Edmund Ignatius Rice)*

**Worthily praise your holy name**

Lord God, to whom every heart is open, every desire known, and from whom no secrets are hidden, purify the thoughts of our hearts by the inspiration of your Holy Spirit, that we may perfectly love you, and worthily praise your holy name. Amen.

*(Gelasian Sacramentary)*

**Work at our common task**

God our Father, you have placed the powers of nature under human control. May we bring the spirit of Christ to all our efforts, and work with our brothers and sisters at our common task, establishing true love, and guiding your creation to perfect fulfilment; through Jesus Christ, your Son, our Lord. Amen.

*(Adapted from the Roman liturgy)*

**God's goodness to me**

I trusted, even when I said, 'I am sorely afflicted,'
and when I said in my alarm, 'No one can be trusted.'

How can I repay the Lord for his goodness to me?
The cup of salvation I will raise; I will call on the Lord's name.

My vows to the Lord I will fulfil before all his people.
Precious in the eyes of the Lord is the death of his faithful.

Your servant, Lord, your servant am I, you have loosened my        bonds.
A thanksgiving sacrifice I make; I will call on the Lord's name.
My vows to the Lord I will fulfil before all his people.

*(Adapted from Psalm 115)*

**Justice and peace**

God the source of truth, lead us, we ask you, in the ways of justice and peace; encourage us, strengthen us to break down all oppression and wrong, to gain for all people their due reward, and from all people their due service, so that each may live for all, and all may care for each; in the name of Jesus Christ our Lord. Amen.

*(Church of Ireland)*

**Fill us from your abundance**
Lord God, life of those who believe in you, glory of the humble and happiness of the saints, listen kindly to our prayer. We long for what you promise; fill us from your abundance; through Christ our Lord. Amen.

*(Adapted from Church of Ireland)*

\* \* \*

*Reflections*

Anyone unwilling to work should not eat. For we hear that some of you are living in idleness, mere busybodies, not doing any work. Now such persons we command and exhort in the Lord Jesus Christ to do their work quietly and to earn their own living.

*(2 Thessalonians 3:10-12)*

Jesus gives all to whoever leaves all.

*(Saint Bernadette Soubirous)*

The best preacher is the heart; the best teacher is time; the best book is the world; the best friend is God.

*(The Talmud)*

## This present moment

Lord God, I thank you for teaching me how to live in the present moment. In this way I enjoy each simple task as I do it, without thinking that I must hurry on to the next thing. I do what I am doing with all my ability and all my concentration. My mind is no longer divided, and life is more peaceful. Thank you for teaching me how to do this. Help me how to show others the way to learn to trust you more completely, and to do everything which has to be done at your time and your speed; in Jesus' name. Amen.

*(Adapted from Michael Hollings and Etta Gullick)*

## Your ways, God, are holy

I cry aloud to God, cry aloud to God that he may hear me.

In the day of my distress I sought the Lord.
At night my hands were raised without ceasing; my soul
    refused to be consoled.
I remember my God and I groaned. I pondered and my spirit
    fainted.

You withheld sleep from my eyes. I was troubled, I could not
    sleep.
I thought of the days of long ago and remembered the years
    long past.
At night I mused within my heart. I pondered and my spir
    it questioned.

'Will the Lord reject us for ever? Will he show us his favour
    no more?
Has his love vanished for ever? Has his promise come to an
    end?
Does God forget his mercy or in anger withhold his compas-
    sion?'

I said, 'This is what causes my grief; that the way of the Most
    High has changed.'
I remember the deeds of the Lord, I remember your wonders
    of old,

I muse on all your works and ponder your mighty deeds.
Your ways, God, are holy. What god is great as our God?
You are the God who works wonders. You showed your
    power among the peoples.
Your strong arm redeemed your people; you guided your
    people like a flock.

*(Adapted from Psalm 76)*

**Blessing**
May the God of peace be with us, taking away our fears and
doubts, and may the mantle of your peace cover those who
are troubled and anxious. May the blessing of peace be upon
us. Amen.

*(Celtic)*

\* \* \*

*Reflections*

All people have, of their very nature, a need to express
themselves in their work and thereby to perfect themselves.
*(Pope John XXIII)*

It is the good use of the present that assures the future.
*(Jean-Pierre de Caussade)*

Everyone who lives and believes in me will never die. Do
you believe this?

*(John 11:26)*

**The Canticle of Brother Sun**

Most high, all-powerful, all good Lord!
All praise is yours, all glory, all honour and all blessing.
To you alone, Most High, do they belong.
No mortal lips are worthy to pronounce your name.

All praise be yours, my Lord, through all that you have made, and first my lord Brother Sun who brings the day; and light you give us through him. How beautiful he is, how radiant in all his splendour! Of you, Most High, he bears the likeness.

All praise be yours, my Lord, through Sister Moon and Stars; in the heavens you have made them, bright and precious and fair.

All praise be yours, my Lord, through Brothers Wind and Air, both fair and stormy, all the weather's moods, by which you cherish all that you have made.

All praise be yours, my Lord, through Sister Water, so useful, lowly, precious and pure.

All praise be yours, my Lord, through Brother Fire, through whom you brighten up the night. How beautiful he is, how free, full of power and strength.

All praise be yours, my Lord, through Sister Earth, our mother, who feeds us in her sovereignty, and produces various fruits with coloured flowers and herbs.

All praise be yours, my Lord, through those who grant pardon for love of you; through those who endure sickness and trial. Happy those who endure in peace; by you, Most High, they will be crowned.

All praise be yours, my Lord, through Sister Death, from whose embrace no mortal can escape. Woe to those who die in mortal sin! Happy those she finds doing your will! The second death can do no harm to them.

Praise and bless my Lord, and give him thanks, and serve him with great humility.

*(Saint Francis of Assisi)*

**Faithful in our responsibilities**
Lord God, who have bound us together in this bundle of life, give us grace to understand how our lives depend upon the courage, the industry, the honesty, and the integrity of our fellow-humans so that we may be mindful of their needs, grateful for their fidelity, and faithful in our responsibilities to them; through Christ our Lord. Amen.

*(Adapted from Reinhold Niebuhr)*

\* \* \*

*Reflections*

So often we demand that others love us without being willing to make the sacrifice and abandonment of self that is necessary to become lovable.

*(John Powell)*

Better is open rebuke than hidden love.

*(Proverbs 27:5)*

None can work well, and love God, and be chaste, except God give it to them.

*(Richard Rolle)*

**Truth and intelligence**

Almighty God, let us commit ourselves wholeheartedly to the truth which brings an everlasting reward, and especially with this end in view that we may intelligently see our obligations, and with intelligence fulfil them. Then the setbacks of life will find us undisturbed, and we ourselves will be found worthy of your heavenly company.

*(From Gregorian Sacramentary)*

**In your mercy look on us**

Almighty Lord God, your glory cannot be approached, your compassion knows no bounds, and your love for all humanity is beyond human expression. In your mercy look on us and all your people; do not leave us to our sins but deal with us according to your goodness. Guide us to the haven of your will and make us truly obedient to your commandments, that we may not feel ashamed when we come before your judgement seat.

For you, God, are good and ever-loving, and we glorify you, Father, Son and Holy Spirit, now and for ever. Amen.

*(Adapted from the Orthodox)*

**For one who is sick**

Lord Jesus Christ, our Redeemer, by the power of the Holy Spirit, ease the sufferings of *(name)*, and make her (him) well again in mind and body. In your loving kindness, forgive *(name)* her (his) sins and grant her (him) full health that she (he) may be restored to your service; through Christ our Lord. Amen.

*(Anon)*

**The blessing of food**

God our Father, the produce of the land is both your gift and the fruit of human work. May our food bring us bodily nourishment, spiritual growth and peace in our homes. May we use your gifts for the good of all; through Christ our Lord. Amen.

*(Pope Paul VI)*

**Continue to the end**

God of compassion, you will that the gate of mercy should always stand open for your people. Look upon us so that we who seek to follow the path of your will may continue in it to the end of our lives; through Christ our Lord. Amen.

*(From Society of Saint Francis)*

**Blessing**

May the God of peace, who brought back from the dead our Lord Jesus, the great shepherd of the sheep, by the blood of the eternal covenant, make us complete in everything good so that we may do his will, working among us that which is pleasing in his sight; through Jesus Christ, to whom be the glory forever and ever. Amen.

*(Adapted from Hebrews 13:20-21)*

* * *

*Reflections*

Salt is good; but if the salt has lost its saltiness, how can you season it?

*(Mark 9:49)*

Carrying our own share of honest doubt is surely part of the journey into a living faith.

*(Wendy Robinson)*

The most important result of our fidelity to prayer is that, despite everything, we want to go on praying.

*(Basil Hume)*

**All I do today**
Heavenly Father, already the morning sun has risen. I ask
that in all I do today, you would keep me from sin and harm.
Control my tongue so that quarrels may not arise. Guard my
eyes from all that is useless. Let the inner depths of my heart
be free from evil. Help me to control myself in food and
drink. When the day draws to a close and night surrounds
me, may I say to you, my God, a prayer of thanks. Amen.

*(Anon)*

**Convert people to you**
Lord Jesus Christ, great shepherd of the flock, who search
for those who are lost, who bind up those who are broken,
and heal those who are sick, we ask you to bless all efforts
that are made to convert people to you. Open people's
minds to hear the words which will bring them peace, and
grant that those whom you raise to the new life of grace may
persevere in it till the end, through your mercy, you who live
and reign with the Father, for ever and ever. Amen.

*(Adapted from the Church of Ireland)*

**God of truth**
From the cowardice that shrinks from new truths,
from the laziness that is content with half-truth,
from the arrogance that thinks it knows all truth,
O God of truth, deliver us.

*(Anon)*

**Your light in our souls**
Lord, in your kindness, pour your light into our souls, so
that we may be devoted to you, by whose wisdom we were
created, and by whose providence we are governed; through
Christ our Lord. Amen.

*(From the Gelasian Sacramentary)*

**I trust you**
God, you have created me to do you some service. You have
given some work to me which you have not given to another. I have my place in your plan: I may never know in this

life what it is but I will know it in the next. Therefore, I trust you in all things: if I am sick, my sickness may serve you; if I am worried, my worries may serve you. You do nothing without purpose; you know what you are doing: you may take away my friends and put me among strangers; you may make me feel forgotten, you may allow my spirits to sink, you may hide my future from me, still, you know what you are doing, and I trust you, Lord. Amen.

*(John Henry Newman)*

\* \* \*

*Reflections*

The Father ... judges all people impartially according to their deeds.

*(Adapted from 1 Peter 1:17)*

As a lantern raises its light in a dark house, so truth rises in the midst of faith in a person's heart. Four darknesses it expels when it rises there: the darkness of paganism, the darkness of ignorance, the darkness of doubt and the darkness of sin, so that none of them can find room there.

*(Colmán mac Beogna)*

Fear is nothing but a giving up of the helps that come from reason.

*(Wisdom 17:12)*

**For those who have lost a partner in life**
Lord, we pray for those who, full of confidence and love, once chose a partner for life, and are now alone after final separation. May they receive the gift of time, so that hurt and bitterness may be redeemed by healing and love, personal weakness by your strength, inner despair by the joy of knowing you and serving others; through Christ our Lord. Amen.

*(Susan Williams)*

**Those who do not acknowledge Christ**
Almighty and eternal God, enable those who do not acknowledge Christ to find the truth as they walk before you in sincerity of heart. Help us to grow in love for one another, to grasp more fully the mystery of your divinity, and to become better witnesses to your love in the sight of all people. We ask this through the same Christ our Lord. Amen

*(Adapted from the Roman liturgy)*

**Those in doubt and uncertainty**
Have mercy, heavenly Father, on those who wander in doubt and uncertainty amid the darkness of this world, and on all who are hardened through sin. Grant them grace to come to themselves, and the will and power to return to you, and to the loving welcome of your forgiveness; through Christ our Lord. Amen.

*(Adapted from the Church of Ireland)*

**Sing a new song to the Lord**
Sing a new song to the Lord for he has worked wonders.
His right hand and his holy arm have brought salvation.

The Lord has made known his salvation; he has shown his
    justice to the nations.
He has remembered his truth and love for his household.

All the ends of the earth have seen the salvation of our God.
Shout to the Lord, all the earth, ring out your joy.

Sing psalms to the Lord with the harp, with the sound of music.

With trumpets and the sound of the horn acclaim the King,
    the Lord.
Let the sea and all within it thunder, the world and all its
    peoples.
Let the rivers clap their hands and the hills ring out their joy.

Rejoice at the presence of the Lord, for he comes to rule the
    earth.
He will rule the world with justice and the peoples with fair-
    ness.

*(Adapted from Psalm 97)*

**Blessing**
Grace be to us and peace from him who is and who was and
who is to come … and from Jesus Christ, the faithful wit-
ness, the first-born of the dead, and the ruler of the kings of
the earth. To him who loves us and freed us from our sins by
his blood, and made us to be a kingdom, priests serving his
God and Father, to him be glory and dominion forever and
ever. Amen.

*(Adapted from Revelation 1:4-6)*

\* \* \*

*Reflections*

What we achieve with toil and labour is, in general, more
perfect and lasting than what we acquire in spiritual sweet-
ness.

*(Saint John of the Cross)*

I dreamed that I was in a village church with a peasant congregation. A man came and stood beside me. I did not turn
towards him, but immediately I felt that this was Christ.
However, when eventually I turned towards him, I saw a
face like anyone else's and clothes on him like anyone else's.
I was astonished, 'What sort of man is this, then? Such an
ordinary, ordinary man.' I was suddenly afraid, but I came
to my senses. Only then did I realise it was just such a face –
a face like all men's faces – that is the face of Christ.'

*(Ivan Turgenyev)*

**The memorial of your suffering and death**
Lord Jesus Christ, you gave us the Eucharist as the memorial of your suffering and death. May our worship of this sacrament of your body and blood help us to experience the salvation you won for us, and the peace of the kingdom where you live with the Father and the Holy Spirit, one God, for ever and ever. Amen.

*(Adapted from the Roman liturgy)*

**Sing praise to our God**
Holy, holy, holy is the Lord God almighty, who was, and
    who is, and who is coming.
Let us praise and glorify him for ever.

Worthy are you, Lord our God, to receive glory and honour
    and power.
Let us praise and glorify him for ever.

Worthy is the Lamb who was slain to receive power and divinity and wisdom and strength and honour and glory and blessing.
Let us praise and glorify him for ever.

Let us bless the Father and the Son and the Holy Spirit.
Let us praise and glorify him for ever.

Bless the Lord, all you works of the Lord.
Let us praise and glorify him for ever.

Praise our God, all you his servants and you who fear him,
    the small and the great.
Let us praise and glorify him for ever.

Praise him in his glory, heaven and earth, and every creature
    that is in heaven and on the earth and under the earth,
    and such as are on the sea, and all that are in them.
Let us praise and glorify him for ever.

Glory be to the Father and to the Son and to the Holy Spirit.
Let us praise and glorify him for ever.
As it was in the beginning, is now, and ever shall be, world
    without end. Amen.
Let us praise and glorify him for ever.

All-powerful, all-holy, most high and supreme God, sovereign good, all good, every good, you who alone are good, it
is to you that we must give all praise, all glory, all thanks, all
honour, all blessing; to you we must refer all good always.
Amen.

*(Saint Francis of Assisi)*

\* \* \*

*Reflections*

To live is to change, and to have changed often is to be perfect.

*(John Henry Newman)*

We must obey God rather than any human authority.

*(Acts 5:29)*

What is best for the Christian life? Simplicity and single-
mindedness. A careless Christianity which resists great
bother, its trial in fire will be great, its reward in heaven will
be small. An active Christianity which resists great comfort,
its trial in fire will be small, its reward in heaven will be
great.
What is best for the mind? Breadth and humility, for every
good thing finds room in a broad, humble mind. What is
worst for the mind? Narrowness and closedness and con-
strictedness, for nothing good finds room in a narrow,
closed, restricted mind.

*(Colmán mac Beogna)*

**Our patron saint**
God our Father, you alone are holy; without you nothing is good. Trusting in the prayers of Saint ( *name*) we ask you to help us to become the holy people you call us to be. Never let us be found undeserving of the glory you have prepared for us. We ask this through Christ our Lord. Amen.

*(Adapted from the Roman liturgy)*

**For those who do not believe in God**
Almighty and eternal God, you created the human race so that all people might long to find you, and have peace when you are found. Grant that, in spite of the hurtful things that stand in their way, people will see in the lives of Christians the signs of your love and mercy, and gladly acknowledge you as the one true God and Father of us all. We ask this through Christ our Lord. Amen.

*(Adapted from the Roman liturgy)*

**Watchful and wakeful**
We ask you, Lord God, to make us watchful and wakeful in waiting for the coming of your Son, Jesus Christ, so that when he stands at the door and knocks he may find us not sleeping in carelessness and sin but awake and rejoicing in his praises; through the same Christ our Lord. Amen.

*(Gelasian Sacramentary)*

**Praise God who is faithful**
My soul, give praise to the Lord.
I will praise the Lord all my days, make music to my God
    while I live.

Put no trust in princes, in mortals in whom there is no help.
Take their breath, they return to clay, and their plans that
    day come to nothing.

They are happy who are helped by God, whose hope is in
    the Lord their God,
Who alone made heaven and earth, the seas and all they
    contain.

God keeps faith for ever, is just to those who are oppressed.
It is God who gives bread to the hungry, the Lord, who sets
   prisoners free,

the Lord who gives sight to the blind, who raises up those
   who are bowed down,
the Lord who protects the stranger, and upholds the widow
   and orphan.

The Lord will reign for ever, the Lord our God from age to
   age.

*(Adapted from Psalm 145)*

**Blessing**
May God our Father and the Lord Jesus Christ give us grace
and peace.

*(Adapted from Romans 1:7)*

* * *

*Reflections*

Why do you persecute me?

*(Acts 9:4)*

What value God places on our loving and keeping peace
with one another! The good Jesus places it before everything
else.

*(Saint Teresa of Avila)*

The best prayer is to rest in the goodness of God, knowing
that that goodness can reach right down to our lowest depths
of need.

*(Julian of Norwich)*

**Christ my shield**
My Christ, my shield, my encircler!
Each day, each night, each dark:
be near me, uphold me, my treasure, my triumph,
in my lying, in my standing, in my watching, in my sleep-
    ing.
Jesus, son of Mary, my helper, my encircler,
Jesus, son of David, my strength everlasting:
Jesus, son of Mary, my helper, my encircler,
Jesus, son of David, my strength everlasting.

*(Adapted from the Celtic)*

**I offer you this day**
My God, I offer you all my thoughts, words, actions and sufferings of this day. I ask you to give me your help so that I
may not offend you but may faithfully serve you and do
your will in all things. Amen.

*(Anon)*

**I place all my trust in you**
Lord Jesus,
if you wish me to be in darkness, may you be blest.
If you wish me to be in light, may you be blest again.
If you are pleased to comfort me, may you be blest.
And if it is your will to punish me, may you also be equally
blest.
Keep me from all sin, and I will fear neither death nor hell.
So long as you do not throw me aside or shut me out from
heaven,
no suffering that comes to me will hurt, because,
Sacred Heart of Jesus, I place all my trust in you.

*(Anon)*

**For those who suffer**
Father, you are the unfailing refuge of those who suffer.
Bring peace and comfort to the sick and the infirm, to the
aged and the dying. Give all those who look after them
knowledge, patience and compassion. Inspire them with

actions which will bring relief, words which will enlighten, and love which will bring comfort. We ask this in Jesus' name. Amen.

*(Adapted from Pope Paul VI)*

### The will of God
May the will of God be done in all of us, and let him do in each of us as seems best and according to his perfect knowledge. Amen.

*(Saint Kentigern)*

\* \* \*

*Reflections*

God's presence is not external to us. It is interior, the presence that makes up and holds together the ground of our being. So we come no longer to *look* for God's presence in the externals of our life but to *recognise* him in them because our eyes are opened interiorly to his indwelling Spirit.

*(Adapted from John Main)*

Put to death, therefore, whatever in you is earthly: fornication, impurity, passion, evil desire, and greed (which is idolatry).

*(Colossians 3:5)*

Do not wish for crosses unless you have borne well those which have already been offered to you. It is a mistake to wish for martyrdom when we do not have the courage to endure a sharp word.

*(Saint Francis de Sales)*

**May my soul thirst for you**
Lord Jesus Christ, pierce my soul with your love so that I may always long for you alone who are the bread of angels and the fulfilment of the soul's deepest desires. May my heart always hunger and feed upon you, so that my soul may be filled with your presence. May my soul thirst for you who are the source of life, wisdom, knowledge, light and all the riches of God our Father. May I always seek you and find you, think of you, speak to you and do all things for the honour and glory of your holy name. Be always my hope, my peace, my refuge and my help in whom my heart is founded, so that I may never be separated from you. Amen.

*(Saint Bonaventure)*

**Give me what I may offer**
Lord, let me offer you the sacrifice of every thought and word; only first give me what I may offer you.

*(Saint Augustine)*

**For those who have died**
Lord, because you are always most merciful and generous with your gifts, look in love on those who have died, especially *(name)*. Because you have loved them from eternity, be merciful and forgive their offences. Cleanse them of their sins, and fulfil their desire to see you face to face in your glory. May they enter into the happiness of the Kingdom prepared for them, there to be united with you for ever and ever. Amen.

*(Anon, from India)*

**I am sorry for my sins**
My God, I am sorry for my sins with all my heart; by sinning I have deserved your punishment. I am sorry because they have offended you who are infinitely good and worthy to be loved above all things. With your help, I intend never to offend you again, and to avoid whatever leads me to sin. Lord, have mercy and forgive me. Amen.

*(Adapted from Pope Paul VI)*

### Salvation through Christ

God our Father, you loved the world so much that you gave your only Son to free us from the ancient power of sin and death. Help us who wait for his coming, and lead us to true liberty; through Christ our Lord. Amen.

*(Adapted from the Roman liturgy)*

### Blessing

Peace be to all of us who are in Christ.

*(Adapted from 1 Peter 5:14)*

\* \* \*

*Reflections*

My God, my God, why have you forsaken me?

*(Mark 15:34)*

Whether we like it or not, whether we know it or not, secretly all nature seeks God and works towards him.

*(Meister Eckhart)*

If we were not expecting that those who had fallen would rise again, it would have been superfluous and foolish to pray for the dead.

*(2 Maccabees 12:44)*

## Holy Virgin Mary

Holy Virgin Mary, among all the women of the world there is none like you; you are the daughter and handmaid of the most high King and Father of heaven; you are the mother of our most holy Lord Jesus Christ; you are the spouse of the Holy Spirit. Pray for us, with Saint Michael the archangel and all the powers of heaven and all the saints, to your most holy and beloved Son, our Lord and Master. Amen.

*(Saint Francis of Assisi)*

## I offer my children to you

Heavenly Father, I offer my children to you. Be their God and Father. Mercifully make up for whatever is missing in me, through weakness, neglect or sin. Deliver them from evil, seen or unseen. Pour your grace into their hearts. Strengthen and increase in them the gifts of your Holy Spirit. May they grow daily in grace and in the knowledge of our Lord Jesus Christ, in whose name we make this prayer. Amen.

*(Dermot Hurley)*

## For the Jews

Almighty and eternal God, long ago you gave your promise to Abraham and his posterity. Listen to your people as we pray that the Jews, the people you first made your own, may arrive at the fullness of redemption. We ask this through Christ our Lord. Amen.

*(Adapted from the Roman liturgy)*

## In time of old age

Lord God, you are the strength of our heart. We ask you not to abandon your servants in the time of their old age when their strength fails, but the more their bodies decline in vigour, so much the more strengthen their souls for the last judgement; through Jesus Christ our Lord. Amen.

*(Adapted from the Church of Ireland)*

**You have redeemed me**

God, you have redeemed me: teach me to love you, so that all my life may be for you, and upheld in you, my Lord, my God.

God, you have redeemed me: draw me to love you; give me the strength, your strength in me, to bear the pains of penitence, to take my cross and follow you, to watch and pray, and to endure to whatever end you have appointed for me, my Lord, my God.

*(Adapted from Gilbert Shaw)*

**Pardon and peace**

Merciful Lord, we ask you to grant your faithful people pardon and peace that they may be cleansed of all their sins and serve you with a quiet mind; through Christ our Lord. Amen.

*(Anon)*

\* \* \*

*Reflections*

The soul has free will: and though the devil can tempt the soul he has not the power to compel it against its will. He suggests to you the idea of fornication; the acceptance or rejection of the suggestion depends on your decision.

*(Saint Cyril of Jerusalem)*

Do not quench the Spirit.

*(1 Thessalonians 5:19)*

The trouble is that we live far from ourselves and have but little wish to get any nearer to ourselves. Indeed we are running away all the time to avoid coming face to face with our real selves, and we barter the truth for trifles.

*(Anonymous Way of a Pilgrim)*

### Acts of faith, hope and charity

My God, I believe in you and all that you teach because you have said it, and your word is true.

My God, I hope in you, for grace and for glory, because of your promises, your mercy and your power.

My God, because you are so good, I wish to love you with all my heart, and, for your sake, to love my neighbour as myself.

*(Anon)*

### Lord, purify our hearts

Lord, purify our hearts and affections through your Holy Spirit, so that our bodies may be chaste and our hearts clean to serve and praise you worthily. Amen.

*(The Roman liturgy)*

### I will not forget your word

How shall the young remain sinless? By obeying your word.
I have sought you with all my heart: let me not stray from
  your commands.
I treasure your promise in my heart lest I sin against you.
Blessed are you, Lord; teach me your statutes.
With my tongue I have recounted the decrees of your lips.
I rejoiced to do your will as though all riches were mine.
I will ponder all your precepts and consider your paths.
I take delight in your statutes; I will not forget your word.

*(Psalm 118:9-16)*

### Holy Mother of God

We turn to you for protection, holy Mother of God.
Listen to us in our prayers and help us in our needs.
Save us from every danger, glorious and blessed Virgin.

  *(From third century, the oldest known prayer to the virgin Mary)*

### Guardian angels

Lord, we ask you to be near us this night. Drive away all evil thoughts. May our guardian angels be with us to keep us in your peace. We ask this through Christ our Lord. Amen.

*(Anon)*

**Blessing**
May the Lord bless us, may he keep us from all evil, and
bring us to everlasting life. Amen.

*(The Roman liturgy)*

\* \* \*

*Reflections*

All scripture is inspired by God, and is useful for teaching,
for reproof, for correction and for training in righteousness.
*(2 Timothy 3:16)*

When we come to heaven, our prayers shall be waiting for
us as part of our delight, with endless joyful thanks from
God.

*(Julian of Norwich)*

Let me take you inside the soul of a rich person without
love, and a wealthy one without friends:
The darkest night, with neither moon nor stars, is like the
brightest day compared with the darkness of this soul.
The coldest winter, with thick snow and hard ice, is like the
warmest summer compared with the coldness of this soul.
The bleakest mountain, bare and swept by gales, is like the
lushest meadow compared with the bleakness of this soul.
You would rather have your body hacked in pieces than
present such a soul as this; you would rather be boiled or
burned alive than suffer such inward torment.

*(Celtic)*

## Be my vision

Be my vision, beloved Lord: none counts for anything but
    the King of the seven heavens.

Be my meditation by day and by night; may it be you that I
    behold for ever in my sleep.

Be my speech; be my understanding; be you for me; and
    may I be for you.

Be my father; may I be your child; may you be mine; and
    may I be yours.

Be alone my special love; let there be none other but the
    High King of heaven.

Your love in my soul and in my heart – grant this to me,
    King of the seven heavens.

Beloved Christ, whatever befalls me, Ruler of all, be my
    vision.

*(Adapted from Celtic)*


## The new and eternal sacrifice

God our Father, we gather to share in the meal which your
only Son left to his people to reveal his love. He gave it to us
when he was about to die, and commanded us to celebrate
it as the new and eternal sacrifice. We pray that in the
Eucharist we may find the fullness of life and love. We ask
this through Christ our Lord. Amen.

*(Adapted from the Roman liturgy)*


## May Christ seal our marriage

May God by whose will the world and all creation have their
being, and who wills the life of all people – may Christ seal
our marriage in the truth of his love. As he finds joy in his
church, so may we find happiness in one another and our
union be strong in love and our coming together be in purity. May his angel guide us, may his peace reign between us,
so that in all things we may be guarded and guided, and we
may give thanks to the Father who will bless us, the Son
who will rejoice in us, and the Spirit who will protect us,
now and for ever. Amen.

*(Adapted from Syrian Orthodox)*

**Hear my prayer**

Please, please, God of my ancestors, Lord of heaven and earth, creator of the waters, king of all creation, hear my prayer. Your strength does not depend on numbers, nor your might on the powerful. But you are the God of the lowly, helper of the oppressed, upholder of the weak, protector of the forsaken, saviour of those without hope.

*(Adapted from Judith 9:12,11)*

**Bless this year**

Lord God, bless this year and bless every kind of fruit, flower and food. Bestow a blessing on the face of the earth, and satisfy your people with your goodness. Bless our years, and make them good years; for your honour and glory. Amen.

*(Adapted from a Polish Jewish Prayer Book)*

\* \* \*

*Reflections*

Come to me, all you that are weary and are carrying heavy burdens, and I will give you rest.

*(Matthew 11:28)*

Daily communion and participation in the holy body and blood of Christ is a good and helpful practice. Christ clearly says, 'The person who eats my flesh and drinks my blood has eternal life.' Who doubts that to partake of life continually is really to have life in abundance? For myself, I communicate four times a week, on the Lord's day, on Wednesday, Friday and Saturday, and on the other days if there is a commemoration of a martyr. If, in times of persecution, individuals, driven by this desire, give themselves communion with their own hands, without the presence of priest or minister, this raises no difficulty.

*(Saint Basil of Caesarea)*

Feed those who are dying of hunger, because if you do not feed them, you are killing them.

*(Gratian, The Decretals)*

### Lord, I believe

Lord, I believe with joy all that is named from of old in the creeds of the gentle apostles. I believe completely because, in your lifetime, you revealed them to us. Every moment of my life I believe in my heart in one God in three persons, the bright eternal Father, the holy Son of peace, and the Holy Spirit who came from them both.

*(Pádraig Ó Callanáin)*

### Holy Spirit, help us

Holy Spirit, help us, weak as we are; we do not know how we ought to pray. See into our hearts, and plead for us in groans that words cannot express. We ask this through Christ our Lord. Amen.

*(Adapted from Romans 8)*

### Rule this heart of mine

Shame on my thoughts, how they stray from me! During the prayers they wander on a path that is not right; they run, they distract, they misbehave before the eyes of the great God … One moment they follow ways of loveliness, and the next, ways of riotous shame – this is no lie! Beloved truly chaste Christ, to whom every eye is clear, may the grace of the sevenfold Spirit come to keep them, to hold them in check! Rule this heart of mine, swift God of the elements, that you may be my love, and that I may do your will!

*(Adapted from Celtic)*

### Pour down your blessings

Lord God, hear our prayers on behalf of Pope *(name)*, our bishop *(name)*, and our parish priest *(name)*. Bless the whole church; convert sinners; have mercy on our country. Pour down your blessings, Lord, on all our relatives, friends and benefactors, and on all who, for any reason, dislike us or do us harm *(name)*. Help the poor and the sick, and especially those who are close to death. God of mercy, have compassion on the souls of the faithful departed, especially *(name)*; grant them, we pray, eternal light, rest and happiness. Amen.

*(Anon, India)*

**The gospel of salvation**

Almighty God, our heavenly Father, who, in your goodness, has caused the light of the gospel to shine among your people, we ask you to extend your mercy to those peoples and places that have still not heard your word. Give them the knowledge of your truth, and grant that the gospel of salvation may be known in all lands, so that the hearts of people may be turned to you; through Jesus Christ our Lord. Amen.

*(Adapted from the Scottish Book of Common Prayer)*

**Blessing**

May peace and mercy be with all the people of God.

*(Adapted from Galatians 6:16)*

\* \* \*

*Reflections*

The Old Testament proclaimed the Father clearly, but the Son obscurely. The New Testament revealed the Son, and gave us a glimpse of the divinity of the Holy Spirit. Now the Spirit dwells among us and grants us a clearer vision of himself.

*(Saint Gregory Nazianzus)*

Do not worry about anything, but in everything by prayer and supplication with thanksgiving let your requests be made known to God. And the peace of God, which surpasses all understanding, will guard your hearts and your minds in Christ Jesus.

*(Philippians 4:6-7)*

The Catholic people, in the length and breadth of Christendom, were the obstinate champions of Catholic truth, and the bishops were not. Perhaps it was permitted, in order to impress upon the church the great evangelical lesson that, not the wise and powerful, but the obscure, the unlearned, and the weak constitute her real strength.

*(Adapted from John Henry Newman)*

**Creator and ruler**
Lord God, creator and ruler of your Kingdom of light, in
your great love for this world you gave up your only Son for
our salvation. His cross has redeemed humanity, his death
has given us life, his resurrection has raised us to glory.
Teach me to be reverent in the presence of your glory; fill my
heart with faith, my days with good works, my life with
your love. May your truth be on my lips and your wisdom
in all my actions, and may I receive the reward of everlasting life; through Christ our Lord. Amen.

*(Anon)*

**Working for justice**
Father, those who work for peace are called your children.
May we never tire of working for that justice which alone
guarantees true and lasting peace; through Christ our Lord.
Amen.

*(Adapted from Pope Paul VI)*

**Acknowledging my selfishness**
Lord God, when I stop and think, I know that I am selfish. I
want things done for me; I want my own way; I demand
from others more than I am prepared to give; I try to use
people; I don't think of the trouble I cause others; I am often
thoughtless and careless of the feelings of others; I often hurt
them because I am thinking of myself and no one else; I am
often ungrateful; I forget how much I owe others and sel-
dom attempt to repay it.
Lord God, make me aware, not just at odd moments, but all
the time how ugly this selfishness is. Fix before my eyes the
example of the cross of Christ, who, though he was rich,
became poor for our sakes. Help me to dethrone myself and
to enthrone him in my heart, so that I may learn from him to
love others rather than myself. This I ask for your love's
sake. Amen.

*(Adapted from William Barclay)*

**Let my soul praise you**

Lord, you change your works but your design is always the same. You are ever old and ever new; yet you give life to all things. Let me offer you the sacrifice of every thought and word; only first give me what I may offer you. Let me not be my own life. I have lived badly on my account and been death to myself, but in you I live again. Speak to me, Lord. Lord my God, let my soul praise you that it may love you. Let it recount to you your mercies that it may praise you for them. Amen.

*(Adapted from Saint Augustine)*

**The souls of your departed servants**

God, you are the creator and redeemer of all the faithful, grant to the souls of your departed servants the remission of all their sins, so that, by the help of our prayers, they may obtain the pardon of their sins as they have always desired; through Christ our Lord. Amen.

*(Anon, from India)*

\* \* \*

*Reflections*

By purifying the soul of all that is not God, God strips us in order to clothe us anew in Christ. Nothing giving place to the All, sorrow is turned into joy.

*(Elizabeth Ruth)*

Faith, by itself, if it has no works, is dead.

*(James 2:17)*

We pray [in the Eucharist] for those who have died, believing that it will be the greatest advantage for the souls of those for whom this supplication is offered when the holy and wonderful sacrifice is set before God.

*(Saint Cyril of Jerusalem)*

**To you be glory**

Father, I bow my knees before you. I pray that, according to the riches of your glory, you may grant that I may be strengthened in my inner being with power through your Spirit.

I pray that Christ may dwell in my heart through faith.

I pray that I may have the power to comprehend, with all the saints, what is the breadth and length and height and depth, and to know the love of Christ that surpasses knowledge, so that I may be filled with all the fullness of God.

Now to you who by the power at work within me are able to accomplish abundantly far more than we can ask or imagine, to you be glory in the church and in Christ Jesus to all generations, forever and ever. Amen.

*(Adapted from Ephesians 3:14-21)*


**In the day of distress I will call**

Turn your ear, Lord, and give answer, for I am poor and needy.
Preserve my life, for I am faithful: save the servant who
    trusts in you.

You are my God, have mercy on me, Lord, for I cry to you all
    the day long.
Give joy to your servant, Lord, for to you I lift up my soul.

Lord, you are good and forgiving, full of love to all who call.
Give heed, Lord, to my prayer and attend to the sound of my
    voice.

In the day of my distress I will call and surely you will reply.
Among the gods there is none like you, Lord, nor work to
    compare with yours.

All the nations shall come to adore you and glorify your
    name, Lord:
for you are great and do marvellous deeds, you who alone
    are God.

Show me, Lord, your way so that I may walk in your truth.
Guide my heart to revere your name.

I will praise you, Lord my God, with all my heart and glorify
    your name for ever;
for your love to me has been great: you have saved me from
    the depths of the grave.

But you, God of mercy and compassion, slow to anger, Lord,
abounding in love and truth, turn and take pity on me.

Give your strength to your servant and save your hand-
    maid's son.
Show me a sign of your favour that you console me and give
    me your help.

*(Adapted from Psalm 85)*

**Blessing**
May the God of peace be with all of us. Amen.
*(Adapted from Romans 15:33)*

\* \* \*

*Reflections*

Prayer is the breathing of the soul; prayer is our spiritual
food and drink. Believe and trust that, as it is easy for you to
breathe the air and live by it, or to eat and drink, so it is easy
and even still easier for your faith to receive all spiritual gifts
from the Lord.

*(John of Kronstadt)*

The Lord is good, a stronghold in a day of trouble; he protects those who take refuge in him.

*(Nahum 1:7)*

Without a renewed education in solidarity, an over-emphasis
on equality can give rise to an individualism in which each
one claims rights without wishing to be answerable for the
common good.

*(Pope Paul VI, Octogesima Adveniens)*

### To think and to do

Lord, grant us, we ask you, the spirit to think and to do what is right, so that we, who cannot do anything that is good without you, may by you be enabled to live according to your will; through Jesus Christ our Lord. Amen.

*(Adapted from the Leonine Sacramentary)*

### The Holy Spirit

Father, you sent the Holy Spirit into my heart, making me one of your children and an heir of your kingdom. You constantly renew my spirit in the sacraments of your redeeming love, freeing me from slavery to sin, and transforming me ever more closely into the likeness of your beloved Son. Thank you for the wonders of your mercy. Glory to you through Christ, in the Holy Spirit, now and for ever. Amen.

*(Anon)*

### The unity of your family

Lord God, you made humanity in your own likeness and you love all that you have made; teach us the unity of your family and the breadth of your love. By the example of Jesus Christ your Son, our Saviour, enable us, while loving and serving our own, to enter into solidarity with the human family. Do not allow us through racial pride, arrogance, or hardness of heart to despise any of those for whom Christ died, or to injure or offend anyone in whom he lives. We ask this for his own name's sake. Amen.

*(Adapted from the Church of Ireland)*

### Increase what you have begun

Humanity in its weakness can never be endowed with the nobler gifts which it may possess unless its first steps are guided by you, our Master. Do you, then, Lord, prepare our minds for the good that you would advance in us, and increase what you have begun. Let us, at all times, give our thoughts to the progress of your kingdom through Christ our Lord. Amen.

*(Adapted from an African collect, fifth century)*

### Use our intelligence

Lord God, you bid us deepen our appreciation of heavenly things through the teaching of the gospel, so raising our thoughts to heaven where Jesus, the Saviour of the world, is ascended. Grant to us who pray, that we may use our intelligence about the many things that come before us, so that when he comes again we may meet him, enriched with the gifts which you have promised to those who believe in you.

*(Adapted from the Gothic Missal)*

\* \* \*

*Reflections*

Many waters cannot quench love, neither can floods drown it. If one offered for love all the wealth of the house, it would be utterly scorned.

*(Song of Solomon 8:7)*

Work is human only if it remains intelligent and free.

*(Pope Paul VI)*

Humanity is still imprisoned in its narrow loyalties.

*(Pierre Teilhard de Chardin)*

**I will lie down in peace**
When I call, answer me, God of justice;
from anguish you released me, have mercy and hear me.

How long, people, will your hearts be closed, will you love
what     is futile and seek what is false?
It is the Lord who grants favours to those whom he loves;
    the Lord hears me whenever I call.

Revere God; do not sin: ponder on your bed and be still.
Make justice your sacrifice and trust in the Lord.
'What can bring us happiness?' many say.
Lift up the light of your face on us, Lord.

You have put into my heart a greater joy than they have from
    abundance of corn and new wine.
I will lie down in peace and sleep comes at once for you
alone,
Lord, make me dwell in safety.

*(Adapted from Psalm 4)*

**Hope, the anchor of our souls**
Lord God, you never forsake those who hope in you. Grant
that we may ever keep that hope which you have given us
by your word as an anchor of our souls, to preserve us sure
and steadfast, unshaken and secure in the storms of life;
through Jesus Christ our Lord. Amen.

*(Anon)*

**Our brothers and sisters who are ill**
Father, your only Son took upon himself the sufferings and
weaknesses of all humanity; through his passion and cross
he taught us how good can be brought out of suffering. Look
upon our brothers and sisters who are ill. In their illness and
pain, may they be united with Christ, who heals both body
and soul; may they know the consolation promised to those
who suffer, and may they be restored to health as you will;
through Christ our Lord. Amen.

*(Adapted from Pope Paul VI)*

**A doorway to hope**

Almighty Father, Son and Holy Spirit, eternal ever blessed gracious God, allow me, the least of the saints, to keep a door in paradise, that I may keep the smallest door, the furthest, the darkest, coldest door, the door that is least used, the stiffest door, as long as it is in your house, Lord God, as long as I can see your glory even from afar, and hear your voice, and know that I am with you, God, for ever. Amen.

*(Attributed to Saint Colmcille)*

**Blessing**

The grace of the Lord Jesus Christ be with us.

*(Adapted from Philemon 25)*

\* \* \*

*Reflections*

See, I have set before you today life and prosperity, death and adversity. If you obey the commandments of the Lord your God that I am commanding you today, by loving the Lord your God, walking in his ways, and observing his commandments, decrees, and ordinances, then you shall live and become numerous, and the Lord your God will bless you.

*(Adapted from Deuteronomy 30:15-16)*

By prayer, the soul is attuned to God.

*(Julian of Norwich)*

Remember, Christian soul, that you have this day and every day of your life God to glorify, Jesus to imitate, a soul to save, a body to mortify, sins to repent of, virtues to acquire, hell to avoid, heaven to gain, eternity to prepare for, time to profit by, neighbours to love, evils to combat, passions to subdue and judgment to undergo.

*(From Gilbert Shaw)*

### Acts of faith, hope and charity

My God, I believe that you are the one God in three divine persons, Father, Son and Holy Spirit. I believe all that you teach because your word is true.

My God, I trust in your goodness and promises. I hope to be forgiven my sins, to be helped by you and to be taken to heaven through the power and goodness of Jesus Christ, my Lord and Saviour.

My God, I wish to love you above all things with all my heart because you are so good. For your sake I will try to love others as I love myself. Amen.

*(Anon)*

### The power of your strength

Lord God, the sovereign good of the soul, you look for our love; deliver us from all sloth in your service and from cold-ness in your cause. Grant us the fire of your love and the power of your strength; through Jesus Christ our Lord. Amen.

*(Adapted from the Church of Ireland)*

### Strength of mind

We humbly ask your Majesty not to allow us to be dispirit-ed by unjust and wounding remarks, nor misled by decep-tive praise. Rather, give us strength of mind to be grateful to those who tell us the truth more than those who insincerely flatter us.

*(Adapted from the Leonine Sacramentary)*

### Prayer of one in distress

With all my voice I cry to the Lord, with all my voice I
    entreat the Lord.
I pour out my trouble before him; I tell him all my distress
    while my spirit faints within me.
But you, Lord, know my path.

On the way where I shall walk they have hidden a snare to
    entrap me.
Look on my right and see: there is no one to take my part.
I have no means of escape, not one who cares for my soul.

I cry to you, Lord. I have said 'You are my refuge, all I have
    in the land of the living.'
Listen, then, to my cry, for I am in the depths of distress.

Rescue me from those who pursue me, for they are stronger
    than I.
Bring my soul out of this prison and then I shall praise
    your name.
Around me the just will assemble because of your goodness
    to me.

*(Adapted from Psalm 141)*

\* \* \*

*Reflections*

Be careful, then, how you live, not as unwise people, but as
wise, making the most of time … Do not be foolish, but
understand what the will of the Lord is.

*(Adapted from Ephesians 5:15-17)*

Happiness is joy in the truth.

*(Saint Augustine)*

God leads every soul by a separate path.

*(Saint John of the Cross)*

### Lonely people

Father, we pray for all lonely people, especially those who, coming home to an empty house, stand in the doorway hesitant and afraid to enter. May all who stand in any doorway with fear in their hearts, like the two disciples on the road to Emmaus, ask the Living One in. Then, by his grace, may they find that in loneliness they are never alone, and that he peoples empty rooms with his presence.

*(Adapted from E. M. Farr)*

### Courage, wisdom and power

Take from us, Lord God, all pride and vanity, all boasting and assertiveness, and give us the courage that shows itself in gentleness, the wisdom that shows itself in simplicity, and the power that shows itself in modesty and thought for others; through Christ our Lord. Amen.

*(Adapted from the Church of Ireland)*

### For grace and deliverance

Lord, give us your grace and deliver us from sin, so that, by your mercy, we may attain the joys of heaven. We ask this in Jesus' name. Amen.

*(From the Sarum Breviary)*

### Peace on earth

Almighty God and Father of all humanity, we ask you to turn to yourself the hearts of all peoples and rulers, so that, by the power of your Holy Spirit, peace may be established on the foundations of justice and truth, through him who was lifted up on the cross to draw all people to himself, your Son Jesus Christ our Lord. Amen.

*(Adapted from the Church of Ireland)*

### I take refuge in you

Preserve me, God, I take refuge in you.
I say to the Lord, 'You are my God; my happiness lies in you
    alone.'

Lord, it is you who are my portion and cup; it is you yourself who are my prize.
The lot marked out for me is my delight; welcome indeed
the heritage that falls to me!

I will bless the Lord who give me counsel, who even at night
directs my heart.
I keep the Lord ever in my sight; since he is at my right hand
I shall stand firm.

And so my heart rejoices, my soul is glad; even my body
shall rest in safety.
For you will not leave my soul among the dead, nor let
your beloved know decay.

You will show me the path of life, the fullness of joy in
your presence,
at your right hand happiness for ever.

*(Adapted from Psalm 15)*

**Blessing**
The grace of the Lord Jesus be with everyone. Amen.

*(Adapted from Revelation 22:21)*

*         *         *

*Reflections*

Pride goes before destruction, and a haughty spirit before a
fall.

*(Proverbs 16:18)*

There is no greater valour nor sterner fight than for self-
effacement, self-oblivion.

*(Meister Eckhart)*

True inner prayer is to stop talking and to listen to a word-
less voice of God within our heart; it is to cease doing things
on our own and enter into the action of God.

*(Kallistos Ware)*

### Let me not neglect God's call

May God open my ears to his call, my eyes to his presence, my heart to his love and my will to his ways. He calls me to make him known to everyone I meet. Let me not neglect this call because I have only one chance, one life to fulfil this mission. Amen.

*(Anon)*

### One in faith and love

God our Father, bring the hearts of all believers together in praise of you and in seeking renewal and reconciliation. May the divisions between Christians be overcome. Make us one in faith and love as walk we with Christ to the joy of your eternal kingdom; through the same Christ our Lord. Amen.

*(Adapted from Pope Paul VI)*

### The praise of God

Revere the Lord and give him honour. Worthy is the Lord to receive praise and honour. All you who revere the Lord, praise him. Heaven and earth, praise him. All you rivers, praise the Lord. All you children of God, praise the Lord. This the day the Lord has made, let us rejoice and be glad in it. Let every spirit praise the Lord. Praise the Lord because he is good; all you who read this, bless the Lord. All you creatures, bless the Lord. All you birds of heaven, praise the Lord. All you children, praise the Lord. Young men and virgins, praise the Lord. Worthy is the Lamb who was slain to receive praise, glory and honour. Blessed be the Holy Trinity and undivided Unity.

*(Attributed to Saint Francis of Assisi)*

### You created the world

Most glorious Lord God, you created the world and you uphold it in marvellous beauty and order, give us grace so to meditate on your power and wisdom, your love and mercy, that we may ever thank you, adore you, and praise you for ever; through Jesus Christ our Lord. Amen.

*(Adapted from the Church of Ireland)*

**Preserve us this day**

Lord, uphold me this day. Strengthen me to bear whatever it brings, whether fulfilment or frustration, support or opposition, acceptance or rejection; through Jesus Christ our Lord and loving Saviour. Amen.

*(Anon)*

**From old life to new life**

Father of love, source of all blessings, help us to pass from our old life of sin to the new life of grace. Prepare us for the glory of your kingdom; through Christ our Lord. Amen.

*(Adapted from the Roman liturgy)*

\* \* \*

*Reflections*

We offer every day, making a memorial of his death. This is one sacrifice, not many. And why? Because it was offered once. We always offer the same person: therefore it is one sacrifice. By the same token, the offering of the sacrifice in many places does not, of course, mean that there are many Christs. Christ is everywhere one, entire in this place and in that, one body, and so, one sacrifice. We offer now what was offered then. We offer the same sacrifice: or rather we make a memorial of that sacrifice.

*(Adapted from Saint John Chrysostom on the Eucharist)*

Eliminate what is obsolete; retain what is useful; determine what is necessary.

*(Pope Paul VI)*

God created humankind in his image, in the image of God he created them; male and female he created them … God saw everything that he had made, and indeed, it was very good.

*(Genesis 1:27,31)*

## Union with you

Grant me a clean heart to see you, detachment of spirit to
serve you, and true recollection to know you. Conform my
spirit to your blessed human nature. Conform my soul to
your holy soul. Conform my body to your pure body. Free
me from all that prevents my union with you. Grant me in
my soul to know you clearly, to love you ardently, to cling to
you in closest union, and to rest in you, not for any merit of
my own, but for the praise of your name. Amen.

*(Adapted from Gilbert Shaw)*

## From a concentration camp

Peace to all those of evil will. Let there be an end to demands
for punishment and retribution. Crimes have surpassed all
measure and can no longer be grasped by human understanding. There are too many martyrs. So, Lord, do not
weigh their sufferings on the scales of justice, nor lay those
sufferings to the torturers' charge to exact a terrible reckon-
ing from them. Pay them back in a different way. Put down
in favour of the executioners, the informers, the traitors and
all those of evil will, the courage, the spiritual strength of
others, their humility, their lofty dignity, their constant inner
striving and their invincible hope. Put down in their favour
the smile, the stench, the tears, the love, the ravaged broken
hearts that remained constant and faithful in the face of
death itself, yes, even at the moment of utmost weakness.
Let all this, Lord, be laid before you for the forgiveness of
sin, a ransom for the triumph of righteousness. Let the good,
not the evil, be taken into account, and may we remain in
our enemies' memory, not as their victims, not as their night-
mare, not as a haunting ghost, but as helpers in their striving to wipe out the fury of their criminal passion. There is
nothing more that we want of them.

*(Adapted from an anonymous note left on the body of a dead
child in Ravensbrück concentration camp in World War II)*

## Give life to the souls of all of us

We ask you, Lover of humanity, to bless all your people.
Send into our hearts the peace of heaven, and grant us also

peace in this life. Give life to the souls of all of us, and let no sin prevail against us or against any of your people. Deliver all who are in trouble, for you are our God, and you set captives free, you give hope to the hopeless, you help the helpless, you lift up the fallen, you are the haven of those in distress. Give your pity, pardon and refreshment to every soul, whether in affliction or error. Preserve us from hurt and danger in our pilgrimage through this life, and grant that we may end our life as Christians, pleasing to you, and free from sin, so that we may enjoy the company of the angels and saints; for the sake of Jesus Christ our Lord and Saviour. Amen.

*(Adapted from the liturgy of Saint Mark)*

**Blessing**
Amen! Blessing and glory and wisdom and thanksgiving and honour and power and might be to our God for ever and ever. Amen.

*(Revelation 7:12)*

\* \* \*

*Reflections*

The function of art lies in … providing a window to the infinite for the hungry soul.

*(Pope Pius XII)*

God, be merciful to me, a sinner!

*(Luke 18:13)*

Though faith is above reason, there can never be found a real contradiction or disagreement between them, as both of them originate from the same source of immutable and eternal truth, from the good and great God, and both so help each other that right reason demonstrates, safeguards and defends the truth of faith, while faith frees reason from error, and through the knowledge of divine things enlightens, strengthens and perfects it.

*(From Pope Pius IX)*

**Grant me eternal salvation**

Almighty God, I give you my body and soul for time and eternity. Forgive me all the sins that I have ever committed. I am sorry for them, and I wish to love you. I believe that your divine Son became man and died for my sins. I believe that you have saved me by the blood of the cross. I believe that there are three persons in one God, the Father, the Son and the Holy Spirit. I trust in you, Lord Jesus, to save me. I ask Mary to pray for me now and at the hour of my death. I ask the prayers of my guardian angel and all the saints, and especially my patron, Saint *(name)*. Lord Jesus, grant me eternal salvation so that I may be with you forever in my heavenly home. Amen.

*(Anon, from India, with adaptation)*

**Happy to share**

Among the sleek and wealthy, the poor are regarded as fools.

Once I was wealthy, and flocks of friends thronged to my door; I   grew poor, and none came near.

In summer people wanted to walk in my shadow; now as I pass in my coarse clothes they avoid me.

The person they saw when I was rich was not me, but my wealth; now they see nobody, pretending I no longer exist.

If I were rich again, their eyes would brighten when they saw me, and their arms reach out to embrace me; now they can watch me collapse without lifting a hand to help me.

The world jibes at me because my barns are bare and my house empty; the proud peer down their noses at me, the rich curl their lips.

Lord, let everyone know both poverty and wealth in their lives; then all would be happy to share what they have.

*(Adapted from the Celtic)*

**For those who are suffering**

Father, you are the unfailing refuge of those who suffer. Bring peace and comfort to the sick and infirm, to the aged and the dying. Give all those who look after them knowledge, patience and compassion. Inspire them with actions which will bring relief, words which will enlighten, and love which will bring comfort. We commend to you the disheartened, the rebellious, those torn by temptation or tormented by desire, and those wounded or abused by human ill-will. Lord, pour out on us your spirit of love, understanding and sacrifice; may we then give effective help to the suffering we meet on our way. Help us to answer their cry, for it is our own. Amen.

*(Adapted from Pope Paul VI)*

**For the faithful departed**
Eternal God, have mercy on the faithful departed for whom our Lord and Saviour Jesus Christ died. Amen.

*(Saint Peter Canisius)*

\* \* \*

*Reflections*

Suddenly, when they looked around, they saw no one with them any more, but only Jesus.

*(Mark 9:8)*

An incessant 'progress', never ending in contentment, means a condemnation of all people to a state of irremediable poverty.

*(Ananda Coomaraswamy)*

Growth involves pain, the pain of leaving behind what went before, all that we have been, in favour of what we are summoned to become.

*(John Main)*

**My soul's desire**

My soul's desire is to see the face of God, and to rest in his house.

My soul's desire is to study the scriptures, and to learn the ways of God.

My soul's desire is to be freed from all fear and sadness, and to share Christ's risen life.

My soul's desire is to imitate my King, and to sing his praises always.

My soul's desire is to enter the gates of heaven, and to gaze upon the light that shines for ever.

Dear Lord, you alone know what my soul truly desires, and you alone can satisfy those desires.

*(Celtic)*

**For the dead**

God, our creator and redeemer, by your power Christ conquered death and returned to you in glory. May all your people who have gone before us in faith share his victory and enjoy the vision of your glory for ever, where Christ lives and reigns with you and the Holy Spirit, one God, for ever and ever. Amen.

*(Adapted from the Roman liturgy)*

**My God, make haste to help me**

In you, Lord, I take refuge; let me never be put to shame.

In your justice rescue me, free me; pay heed to me and save me.

Be a rock where I can take refuge, a mighty stronghold to save me, for you are my rock, my stronghold.

Free me from the hand of the wicked, from the grip of the unjust, of the oppressor.

It is you, Lord, who are my hope, my trust, Lord, since my youth.

On you I have leaned from my birth; from my mother's womb you have been my help.

My hope has always been in you.

My lips are filled with your praise, with your glory all the
day long.

Do not reject me now that I am old; when my strength fails
do not forsake me.

For my enemies are speaking about me. They say, 'God has
forsaken him, follow him, seize him; there is no one to
save him.'

God, do not stay far off; my God, make haste to help me.

*(Adapted from Psalm 70)*

**Blessing**
May almighty God bless us, the Father, the Son and the Holy
Spirit. Amen.

\* \* \*

*Reflections*

A pure, clean heart is the temple of God, where the eternal
God lives always in truth, when all that is unlike him has
been driven out.

*(John Tauler)*

We get ready for death by beginning to live life as we should
have been living it all along.

*(Ronald Rolheiser)*

Let it be known to you, therefore … that through this man,
Jesus, forgiveness of sins is proclaimed to you.

*(Adapted from Acts 13:38)*

**God made us a family**
God made us a family. We need one another. We love one another. We forgive one another. We work together. We play together. We pray together.

Together we use God's word. Together we grow in Christ. Together we love all people. Together we serve God. Together we hope for heaven.

These are our hopes and our ideals. God, help us to attain them. Through Jesus Christ our Lord. Amen.

*(Anon)*


**Present and future**
All-powerful and merciful Father, refreshment of the weary, comfort in sorrow, strength in our weakness, hear the prayer which we sinners make to you: save and sustain us in our present need, and help us to face the future with courage; through Christ our Lord. Amen.

*(Adapted from Pope Paul VI)*


**Deliver us**
Lord God, to save us, you gave your Son to death on the cross, and by his glorious resurrection delivered us from the power of the enemy. Grant us to die daily to sin, that we may live closer to him in the joy of the resurrection; through Christ our Lord. Amen.

*(Saint Gregory the Great)*


**I will praise you, Lord**
I will praise you, Lord, you have rescued me and have not
    let my enemies rejoice over me.

Lord, I cried to you for help and you, my God, have healed
    me.
Lord, you have raised my soul from the dead, restored me to
    life from those who sink into the grave.

Sing psalms to the Lord, you who love him, give thanks to
    his   holy name.
His anger lasts but a moment; his favour through life. At
    night there are tears, but joy comes with dawn.

I said to myself in my good fortune, 'Nothing will ever
    disturb me.'
Your favour had set me on a mountain fastness; then you hid
    your face and I was put to confusion.

To you, Lord, I cried, to my God I made appeal, 'What prof
    it would my death be, my going to the grave?
Can dust give you praise or proclaim your truth?'

The Lord listened and had pity. The Lord came to my help.
For me you have changed my mourning into dancing,
you removed my sackcloth and girdled me with joy.

So my soul sings psalms to you unceasingly;
Lord my God, I will thank you for ever.'

*(Psalm 29)*

\* \* \*

*Reflections*

God sends us nothing that is too hard and painful to bear.
He proportions all to our strengths and abilities. Our trials
are suited to our needs as a glove to the hand of the wearer.
All things will contribute to our sanctification if we but
cooperate with the designs of Divine Providence.

*(Saint Alphonsus Liguori)*

We cannot think too little of ourselves, or too much of our
souls.

*(G. K. Chesterton)*

Find the door of the inner room of your soul and you will
discover that this is the door into the kingdom of heaven.

*(Saint John Chrysostom)*

**I believe in God**

I believe in God the Father who created heaven and earth, and in Jesus Christ his Son who was born of the virgin Mary, who suffered torment once under Pontius Pilate, who indeed was tortured high upon a cross. He died because of the sin of Adam and Eve, and went into hell of the sorrows to visit the souls. When the third morning came he rose mighty from the earth, and sits in truth on the right hand of the God of power. From there he comes again riding on the clouds to pass judgment on the dead, and no injustice will he do. I yield further to the Holy Spirit and to Peter's holy church placed fast on a rock never to sway, which the devil and his angels ever try to move and bring down, yet always in vain. I believe truly in the communion of saints and angels, the forgiveness of sins, the resurrection of the dead and in eternity.

*(Adapted from the Celtic)*

**I am growing old**

Lord, you know better than I do that I am growing old and someday will be old. Keep me from the habit of thinking that I must say something on every subject and on every occasion. Release me from the craving to straighten out everyone's affairs. Make me thoughtful but not moody, helpful but not bossy. With my vast store of wisdom, it seems a pity not to use it all, but you know, Lord, that I want a few friends at the end.

Keep my mind free from the recital of endless details; give me wings to get to the point. Seal my lips on my aches and pains. They are increasing, and love of rehearsing them is becoming sweeter as the years go by. I dare not ask for grace enough to enjoy the tales of others' pains, but help me to endure them with patience.

I dare not ask for improved memory, but for a growing humility and a lessening cocksureness when my memory clashes with the memories of others. Teach me the glorious lesson that I may occasionally be mistaken.

Keep me reasonably sweet; I do not want to be a saint –

some of them are so hard to live with – but a sour old person is one of the crowning works of the devil. Give me the ability to see good things in unexpected places, and talents in unexpected people, and give me, Lord, the grace to tell them so. Amen.

*(Attributed to an anonymous seventeenth century nun)*

**Blessing**
In the name of the Father, in the name of the Son, in the name of the Spirit, three in one:
Father, cherish us; Son, cherish us; Spirit, cherish us, three-all-kindly.
Father, make us holy; Christ, make us holy; Spirit, make us holy, three all-holy.
Three, aid my hope; three, aid my love; three, aid our eyes and our knees from stumbling. Amen.

*(Adapted from the Celtic)*

* * *

*Reflections*

We come to the house of faith only after we have travelled through the forest of doubt.

*(Peter Abélard)*

The word 'angel' is the name of an office, not of a nature.
*(Saint Gregory the Great)*

Long ago God spoke to our ancestors in many and various ways by the prophets, but in these last days he has spoken to us by the Son … through whom he also created the worlds.

*(Adapted from Hebrews 1:1-2)*

**A hundred thousand welcomes**

A hundred thousand welcomes, holy Body of Christ; a hundred thousand welcomes, body that was crucified; a hundred thousand welcomes to your body, Lord; only Son of God, hail to you!

You are the branch of all grace, the Tree whose flower never withers, as wrote Matthew and Mark.

God, if you consider us worthy to be accepted, may we live and be saved by your hands.

I ask for grace and mercy for myself and for the race of Eve and Adam, for whom God and the church direct us to pray. Amen.

*(Adapted from Celtic)*

**Confirm our hope**

Father, help us to understand your great love for us. May the goodness you show us through the passion, death and resurrection of Jesus Christ your Son and our saviour confirm our hope in your future mercy. We ask this through Christ our Lord. Amen.

*(Adapted from the Roman liturgy)*

**For our children**

Heavenly Father, we commend our children to you. You are their God and Father. Mercifully make up for whatever is missing in us through weakness or neglect. May we live in such a way as to be an example to them; may we never, through lack of courage or character, fail to point out to them right and wrong. May we give time to them, be with them, listen to them, walk, talk, laugh and share with them. Strengthen them to overcome the evil of the world and to resist temptation to sin. Pour your grace into their hearts. Increase in them the gifts of your Holy Spirit. May they grow daily in grace and in the knowledge of Jesus Christ. May they serve you faithfully here on earth, and rejoice, with us, in your presence for ever in heaven. Amen.

*(Anon)*

**Thank you for food**

Lord, we thank you for the food that the earth produces for the good of humanity. It is evidence of your generosity; may the seeds of charity and justice also bear fruit in our hearts; through Christ our Lord. Amen.

*(Adapted from the Roman liturgy)*

**We thank you, our God**

Blessed are you, Lord, God of our ancestors, forever and ever.

Yours, Lord, are the greatness, the power, the glory, the
    victory, and the majesty;

for all that is in the heavens and on the earth is yours.

Yours is the kingdom, Lord, and you are exalted as head
    above all.

Riches and honour come from you, and you rule over all.

In your hand are power and might; and it is in your hand to
    make great and to give strength to all.

And now, our God, we give thanks to you, and praise your
    glorious name.

*(Adapted from 1 Chronicles 29:10-13)*

\* \* \*

*Reflections*

Neither death, nor life, nor angels, nor rulers, nor things present, nor things to come, nor powers, nor height, nor depth, nor anything else in all creation, will be able to separate us from the love of God in Christ Jesus our Lord.

*(Adapted from Romans 8:38-39)*

The Eucharist is, as it were, the soul of the church.

*(Pope Leo XIII)*

Better is a dinner of vegetables where love is than a fatted ox and hatred with it.

*(Proverbs 15:17)*

**The Holy Trinity**

Almighty and eternal God, we ask you to strengthen our faith so that in this world we may firmly proclaim our faith in the Holy Trinity, and, in the world to come, know you perfectly and with joy look upon you face to face; for you live and reign, one God, for ever and ever. Amen.

*(Adapted from the Society of Saint Francis)*

**Two or three**

Lord God, who has taught us to pray together and has promised that wherever two or three gather in your name you are there among them, hear now our prayers for our salvation, and give us in this world knowledge of your truth, and, in the world to come, life everlasting; for the sake of Jesus Christ our loving Saviour. Amen.

*(Adapted from the Armenian liturgy)*

**Help our bishop**

God, eternal shepherd, you tend your church in many ways, and you care for us with love. Help our bishop *(name)*, whom you have chosen to be pastor for Christ, to watch over his people. Help him to be a holy priest and a wise administrator. We make this prayer through Christ our Lord. Amen.

*(Adapted from the Roman liturgy)*

**Our Father**

Our Father in heaven, may you receive the adoration due to you;

May all peoples, everywhere, listen to you and do what you want them to do.

May your saving power be effective everywhere.

Give us each day whatever we need for body, mind and soul.

Forgive us the wrongs we have done, as we forgive those who have wronged us.

Do not allow us to yield to temptation but deliver us from evil. Amen.

*(Adapted from R. H. Lesser)*

**Christ yesterday and today**

Christ yesterday and today, the beginning and the end, the Alpha and the Omega; all time belongs to him, and all the ages; to him be glory and power, through every age and for ever. Amen.

*(Adapted from the Roman liturgy)*

**Blessing**

May our God and Father himself and our Lord Jesus direct our way.

May the Lord make us increase and abound in love for one another and for all.

May he so strengthen our hearts in holiness that we may be blameless before our God and Father at the coming of our Lord Jesus with all his saints.

*(Adapted from 1 Thessalonians 3:11-13)*

\* \* \*

*Reflections*

In silence and solitude ... one is occupied in busy leisure and rests in quiet activity.

*(Saint Peter Damian)*

See what love the Father has given us, that we should be called children of God; and that is what we are. We are God's children now; what we will be has not yet been revealed. What we know is this: when he is revealed, we will be like him, for we will see him as he really is.

*(Adapted from 1 John 3:1-2)*

Take no oath by the earth that you stand on. You walk on it only for a while, but soon you will be buried within it. Pay no heed to the world you live in. You are dazzled by its pomp and pleasure, but soon you shall be carried from it. Time is like the ebbing tide on a beach. You cannot see it move by staring at it, but soon it has run away from sight.

*(Celtic)*

**I turn to you and pray**

Lord our God, I turn to you and pray, knowing that you are near, that you may have mercy on me and abundantly pardon. For my thoughts are not your thoughts, nor are my ways your ways. For as the heavens are higher than the earth, so are your ways higher than my ways and your thoughts than my thoughts. Lord, hear my prayer.

*(Adapted from Isaiah 55:6-9)*

**My whole day**

Lord Jesus, I offer you my whole day, my work, my hopes, my fight against sin, my joys and sorrows. Give me and those who work with me the grace to think like you, to work with you, to live with you. May we love you with all our hearts and serve you with all our strength. May your kingdom come in factories, shops, farms, offices and homes. May you be better known, loved and served. May those of us today who may be tempted to leave you by sin remain in your grace. Amen.

*(Adapted from Young Christian Workers' prayer)*

**When we are tired**

God, you are the strength of those who labour and the rest of the weary. Grant that when we are tired by our work we may be renewed and re-created by your Spirit to serve you gladly in freshness of body and mind; through Jesus Christ our Lord. Amen.

*(Adapted from the Church of Ireland)*

**Make me your own**

My God, I am not my own but yours. Take me for your own and help me in all things to do your holy will. God, I give myself to you in joy and sorrow, in sickness and health, in success and failure, in life and death, in time and eternity. Make me and keep me your own; through Jesus Christ our Lord. Amen.

*(Anon)*

**The source of intelligence**
Lord, you are the source of intelligence and right thinking.
So as to train and establish us in true wisdom, teach us first
to have reverence, and then perfect us in clear thinking; in
Jesus' name. Amen.

*(Adapted from the Gothic Breviary)*

**Grant us your help today**
Lord God, you have given us the earth to cultivate and care
for; you give us talents and abilities to nurture. Grant us
your help today to work faithfully for your glory and for
the good of others. Amen.

*(Anon)*

\* \* \*

*Reflections*

By this we may be sure that we know him, if we obey his
commandments. Whoever says, 'I have come to know him,'
but does not obey his commandments, is a liar, and in such
a person the truth does not exist; but whoever obeys his
word, truly in this person the love of God has reached perfection. By this we may be sure that we are in him: whoever
says, 'I abide in him,' ought to walk just as he walked.

*(Adapted from 1 John 2:3-6)*

When I see people very anxious to know what sort of prayer
they practise … I know how little they understand how to
attain union with God, since they think it consists in things
such as these. No. Our Lord expects *works* from us! If you see
someone sick whom you can relieve, never fear losing your
devotion, but have compassion on her; if she is in pain, feel
it as if it were your own … This is the true union of our will
with the will of God. If you possess charity, I assure you that
you will attain the union I have described.

*(Adapted from Saint Teresa of Avila)*

**Sounding silence**

Lord, the scripture says, 'There is a time for silence and a time for speech.' Teach me the silence of humility, the silence of wisdom, the silence of love, the silence that speaks without words and the silence of faith. Lord, teach me to silence my own heart that I may listen to the gentle movement of the Holy Spirit within me and sense the depths which are of God. Amen.

*(Anon, sixteenth century)*

**Those who feel rejected**

My God, help all who feel rejected, those who have lost their job or who cannot get one, those who are abandoned or ignored, those whose love is spurned. Make them aware of your love and help them to realise that what matters is to love more than to be loved. And take away, Lord, my own sense of rejection or despair. Amen.

*(Anon)*

**Walk in justice**

Hear, you who are far away, what I have done; and you who are near, acknowledge my might.

Those who walk righteously and speak uprightly, who despise the gain of oppression, who wave away a bribe instead of accepting it, who stop their ears from hearing of bloodshed and shut their eyes from looking on evil, they will live on the heights; their refuge will be the fortresses of rocks; their food will be supplied, their water assured.

*(Adapted from Isaiah 33:13, 15-16)*

**Love our country**

Lord God, by whose will we live in this land, enable us to love our country, not in word only, but in deed and in truth. Let the strong give according to their ability so that the weak may receive according to their need, in the spirit of Jesus your Son who came not to be served but to serve, he who is our Lord for ever and ever. Amen.

*(Church of Ireland)*

**The joy of lasting peace**
God and Father, light of all humanity, make our hearts radiant with the splendour of that light which long ago you shed on our ancestors in the faith, and give your people the joy of lasting peace; through Christ our Lord. Amen.

*(Adapted from the Roman liturgy)*

**Blessing**
May the everlasting Father bless us with his everlasting blessing. Amen.

*(Adapted from Thomas Cranmer)*

\* \* \*

*Reflections*

Wherever people are praying in the world, there the Holy Spirit is, the living breath of prayer.

*(Pope John Paul II, Dominum et Vivificantem)*

To do righteousness and justice is more acceptable to the Lord than sacrifice.

*(Proverbs 21:3)*

We must live today; those who live tomorrow never live. If we want to live today, we should live for God, in whom yesterday and tomorrow are nothing but today.

*(Adapted from Marsiglio Ficino)*

**Let the Spirit do the rest**

Sometimes when I pray, I speak the words, but I do not feel or think them.

Sometimes when I pray, I speak the words, thinking about what I say, but not feeling.

Sometimes when I pray, I speak the words, and I both think and feel what I say.

An act of will cannot make me feel, nor stop my mind from wandering.

An act of will can only make me speak, so I shall speak the words,

and let the Spirit do the rest, guiding my mind and heart as he wills. Amen.

*(Celtic)*

**Open our lips**

God and Father of our Lord Jesus Christ, you have called us from sleep and brought us to this hour of prayer. Open our lips and inspire us with your grace; accept the thanksgiving that we lift to you as well as we can, and teach us to do your will, for we cannot pray as we should unless, Lord, you guide us through your Holy Spirit. And so we pray: if we have sinned in thought, word or deed, whether deliberately or in weakness, will you forgive, remit and pardon all our sins, for if you, Lord, kept a record of our sins, who could stand it? But with you there is forgiveness and deliverance; you alone are the holy one, our help, our refuge and our defence, and our songs of praise will be always and only yours.

For we celebrate in glory and blessing the power of your majesty, Father, Son and Holy Spirit, now and for ever, to the ages of ages. Amen.

*(Adapted from the Orthodox)*

**Unity and peace**

Lord, holy Father, faithful to your promise you sent your Spirit to bring together a people divided by sin. Give us grace to foster unity and peace among people; through Christ our Lord. Amen.

*(Adapted from the Roman liturgy)*

## Grace upon grace

God our Father, let us find grace in your sight so as to have grace to serve you acceptably with reverence and respect, and still more grace not to receive your grace in vain, not to neglect it and fall from it, but to persevere in it till the end of our lives; through Jesus Christ our Lord. Amen.

*(Adapted from Lancelot Andrewes)*

## The fulfilment of all our hopes

Give me, good and kindly Father, intelligence to know you and a lively awareness of you. Grant me, also, a mind that can appreciate you, diligence in looking for you and wisdom to recognise you. Let there be in me the desire to love you and to think of you often, and enthusiasm in working for you while being ever alert to your guidance. Give me words in which to speak of you. May I be unfailingly patient in waiting for you, for you are the fulfilment of all our hopes. Amen.

*(Alcuin)*

\* \* \*

*Reflections*

Rejoice always, pray without ceasing, give thanks in all circumstances; for this is the will of God in Christ Jesus for you.

*(1 Thessalonians 5:16-18)*

We are in a world where the fundamental question for each individual has to be, 'Do I believe?', where the unattended hunger of the soul is the stalking famine of the emerging generation.

*(Niall Ahern)*

God is truth. All who seek truth seek God, whether this is clear to them or not.

*(Saint Edith Stein)*

**We offer you our thanksgiving**

Almighty and eternal God, in your great love for the human race you have brought us at this hour into the presence of your glory to sing in praise of your wonderful works; look with favour on us your servants, and grant that with a contrite heart we may faithfully sing, 'Holy, holy, holy Lord' and offer you thanksgiving for the great gifts that you continually bestow on us. Remember our weakness, Lord, and do not cast us out on account of our sins: look with compassion on our condition, so that shunning the darkness of sin we may walk in the light of your justice, and that having put on the armour of light we may pass our lives safe from every temptation and evil, and so give you glory in all things, knowing that you are our Father, you who are the one true God, abounding in love for all humanity.

For you, Lord, are the holy one, and we glorify you, Father, Son and Holy Spirit, now and for ever to the ages of ages. Amen.

*(Adapted from the Orthodox)*


**May we always seek your face**

Lord, grant us to be clean in our speech, our hearts and our actions; give us humility, patience, self-control, prudence, justice and courage; give us the spirit of wisdom and understanding, the spirit of counsel and strength, the spirit of knowledge and godliness, and of reverence for you; may we always seek your face with all our heart, all our soul and all our mind; grant us to have a contrite and humbled heart in your presence, preferring nothing to your love. Have mercy on us, we ask you; through Jesus our Lord. Amen.

*(Adapted from the Gallican Sacramentary)*


**Stretch out your hand to heal**

Sovereign Lord, who made the heaven and the earth, the sea and everything in them, stretch out your hand to heal, and grant that signs and wonders be performed through the name of your holy servant Jesus. Amen.

*(Adapted from Acts 4:24,30)*

**Blessing**

I lie down with God; may God lie down with me.

May the right hand of God be under my head and the two
    hands of Mary embrace me.

May the angels of God support me, from the top of my head
    to the soles of my feet.

I will never lie down with evil; may evil never lie down with
    me.

Mary, mother of Jesus, and Elizabeth, mother of John, nurse
    me when I fall sick and restore me to health.

Jesus, nailed to the cross, and John, beheaded by Herod, be
    close to me when I die and carry me to heaven.

Jesus, forgive my sins. Amen.

*(Celtic)*

\* \* \*

*Reflections*

Nothing should alienate us from one another but what alien-
ates us from God.

*(Benjamin Whichcote)*

Lord, you have the words of eternal life. We have come to
believe and know that you are the Christ, the Son of the living God.

*(Adapted from John 6:68-9)*

For those who truly desire a life of prayer, the only way to
achieve it is by prayer.

*(Mother M. Clare)*

**I will bless the Lord**

I will bless the Lord at all times, his praise always on my
    lips;
in the Lord my soul shall make its boast; the humble shall
    hear and be glad.

Glorify the Lord with me; together let us praise his name.
I sought the Lord and he answered me; from all my terrors
    he set me free.

Look towards him and be radiant; let your faces not be
abashed.
The poor called and the Lord heard them and rescued them
    from all their distress.

The angel of the Lord is encamped around those who revere
    him, to rescue them.
Taste and see that the Lord is good; they are happy who seek
    refuge in him.

*(Adapted from Psalm 33:2-9)*


**Remember your servants**

Lord, remember those who have braved dangers and suffered hardship for your name's sake in advancing the cause
of truth. Remember those who, in their time, founded
Christian communities, and built them up in your name.
You cannot forget the many who have borne persecution
and pain for the truth and so brought wandering souls back
to you; nor those who have carried the cross to new lands
and peoples and caused your name to be praised among
them. By their prayers and works, raise us all closer to yourself, and open our minds to the fullness of your truth.

*(Liturgy of Philoxenus)*


**You are blessed, Lord God**

Blessed are you, Lord, God of our ancestors;
    to you glory and praise for evermore.
Blessed is your glorious, holy name;
    to you glory and praise for evermore.
Blessed are you in the temple of your holy glory;
    to you glory and praise for evermore.

Blessed are you who look into the depths;
  to you glory and praise for evermore.
Blessed are you on the throne of your kingdom;
  to you glory and praise for evermore.
Blessed are you in the firmament of heaven;
  to you glory and praise for evermore.
Blessed are you in all your works;
  to you glory and praise for evermore.
May the heavens sing praise to you;
  to you glory and praise for evermore.
May all the angels highly exalt you for ever,
  to you glory and praise for evermore.
Blessed are you, Lord, God of our ancestors;
  to you glory and praise for evermore.

*(Adapted from Daniel 3:52-59)*

**May the Trinity protect me**
The path I walk, Christ walks it. May the land in which I am
be without sorrow. May the Trinity protect me wherever I
stay, Father, Son and Holy Spirit. Bright angels walk with
me, and be present with me in every dealing.

*(Attributed to Saint Colmcille)*

\* \* \*

*Reflections*

God did not give us a spirit of cowardice, but rather a spirit
of power and of love and of self-discipline.

*(2 Timothy 1:7)*

It is impossible to cheat reality; reality will always take its
revenge.

*(Jean Sulivan)*

You can't safely know more about God than you know about
yourself.

*(Rabbi Lionel Blue)*

**Come, ring out your joy**

Happy are they whose offence is forgiven, whose sin is remitted.

Happy are they to whom the Lord imputes no guilt, in whose spirit is no guile.

I kept my sin secret and my frame was wasted, I groaned all the day long, for night and day your hand was heavy upon me.

Indeed, my strength was dried up as by the summer's heat.

But now I have acknowledged my sins, my guilt I did not hide.

I said, 'I will confess my offence to the Lord,'

and you, Lord, have forgiven the guilt of my sin.

You are my hiding place, Lord, you save me from distress, you surround me with cries of deliverance.

Rejoice, rejoice in the Lord; exult, you just! Come, ring out your joy, all you upright of heart!

*(Adapted from Psalm 31)*

**Forgive my sins**

Forgive the sins that I can remember and also the sins I have forgotten.

Forgive the wrong actions I have committed and the right actions I have omitted.

Forgive the times that I have been weak in the face of temptation and those when I have been stubborn in the face of correction.

Forgive the times when I have been too proud of my achievements and those when I have failed to boast of your works.

Forgive the harsh judgments I made of others and the leniency I have shown to myself.

Forgive the lies I have told to others and the truths I have avoided.

Forgive the pain I have caused others and the indulgence I have shown myself.

Jesus, have pity on me and make me whole. Amen.

*(Celtic)*

**The serenity prayer**
God grant me the serenity to accept the things I cannot change, courage to change the things I can, and wisdom to know the difference.

*(From Reinhold Niebuhr)*

**Blessing**
The wisdom of the wonderful Counsellor guide us; the strength of the mighty God defend us; the love of the everlasting Father enfold us, the peace of the Prince of Peace be upon us.
And the blessing of God almighty, Father, Son and Holy Spirit be upon us this night and for evermore. Amen.

*(Anon)*

\* \* \*

*Reflections*

Stay with us, because it is almost evening and the day is now nearly over.

*(Luke 24:29)*

The fact that the almighty power of God was able to descend to the lowly condition of humanity provides a clearer proof of power than great and impressive miracles. His descent to our lowliness is the supreme expression of his power.

*(Saint Gregory of Nyssa)*

Our challenge is to cooperate with others while retaining our identity and allowing them to retain theirs.

*(William Johnston)*

## Sing to the Lord

Sing to the Lord, all the earth. Tell of his salvation from day
to day.

Declare his glory among the nations, his marvellous works
among all the peoples.

For great is the Lord, and greatly to be praised; he is to be
revered above all gods.

Honour and majesty are before him; strength and joy are in
his place.

*(1 Chronicles 16:23-25, 27)*

## Bring us together

God of all good, generous giver of tranquillity and peace,
grant that same tranquillity and peace to your people. Heal
the quarrels that exist among us and bring us together in
unity. May we pray earnestly for each other so that the peace
which is from you may be an anchor of faith in our souls.
Amen.

*(Adapted from the liturgy of Maruta of Tikrit)*

## King of creation

My dear King, my own King, without pride or sin, you
created the whole world, eternal, victorious King.

King above the elements and the sun, King beneath the
ocean, King of the north and the south, the east and the west,
against you no enemy can prevail.

King of the mysteries, you existed before the elements,
before the sun was set in the sky, before the waters
covered the ocean floor; beautiful King, you are without
beginning or end.

King, you created the daylight and the darkness; you are not
arrogant or boastful but strong and firm.

King, you created the land out of shapeless mass, you
carved the mountains and chiselled the valleys, and
covered the earth with trees and grass.

King, you stretched out the sky above the earth, a perfect
sphere    like a perfect apple, and you decorated the sky with
stars to shine at night.

King, you pierced the earth with springs from which pure
water flows, to form streams and rivers across the land.

King, you measured each object and each span within the
   universe: the heights of the mountains and the depths of
   the ocean; the distance from the sun to the moon, and
   from star to star.

King, you ordained the movements of every object: the sun
   to cross the sky each day and the moon to rise each night;
   the clouds to carry rain from the sea and the rivers to
   carry water back to the sea.

King, you divided the earth into three: the north, cold and
   bitter; the south, hot and dry; and the middle, cool, wet
   and fertile.

King, you created men and women to be your stewards of
   the earth, always praising you for your boundless love.
Amen.

*(Celtic)*

\* \* \*

*Reflections*

In order to restore communion and unity, or to preserve
them [among Christians], one must impose no burden
beyond what is indispensable.

*(Vatican II, Unitatis Redintegratio)*

See, I am setting before you today a blessing and a curse: the
blessing if you obey the commandments of the Lord your
God that I am commanding you today; and the curse, if you
do not obey the commandments of the Lord your God, but
turn from the way that I am commanding you today, to follow other gods that you have not known.

*(Deuteronomy 11:26-28)*

The deeper one is drawn into God, the more one must go to
the world in order to carry the divine life into it.

*(Saint Edith Stein)*

### Loving and being loved is holiness

Lord God, you have promised a new heart and a new spirit to those who love you. Give me, I pray, a share in the spirit of Jesus your Son and teach me how to live in love. May I abandon myself to you, discovering that I can live free from fear, free from the chains that bind me to myself, to my past, to my sins, to wondering what others will say, because I know I can have confidence in you.

You, Lord, are merciful. You are kind and compassionate; you welcome sinners and forgive them completely. And so I come to you with absolute trust. My God, loving you and being loved by you is holiness. For this gift I hold out my hands. Grant it to me in Jesus' name. Amen.

*(Elizabeth Ruth Obbard)*

### Blessed be God

Blessed are you, merciful God! Blessed is your name forever; let all your works praise you forever. And now, Lord, I turn my face to you and raise my eyes towards you. Blessed are you, God of our ancestors, and blessed is your name in all generations forever. Let the heavens and the whole creation bless you forever. Blessed be God, and blessed be his great name, and blessed be all his holy angels. May his holy name be blest throughout all the ages.

*(Adapted from Tobit 3:11-12; 8:5; 11:14)*

### Into everlasting life

We ask you, Lord, to strengthen us, your servants, in your grace so that, at the hour of death, the enemy may not prevail over us, and we may pass with your angels into everlasting life. Amen.

*(Anon, from India)*

### To please your holy name

Eternal God, King of all creation, who has granted me to reach this hour, forgive me the sins I have committed this day in thought, word and deed. Clean my soul, Lord, from every stain of sin. Grant me to sleep this night in peace, to rise from my bed and praise your holy name all the days of

my life, and to overcome the enemies, both bodily and spiritual, that fight against me. Deliver me, Lord, from foolish
thoughts that deceive me and from evil desires.

For yours is the kingdom, the power and the glory, of the
Father, the Son and the Holy Spirit, now and for ever to the
ages of ages. Amen.

*(Adapted from Saint Makarios the Great)*

**Blessing**

Bless all who worship you, from the rising of the sun to its
setting. Of your goodness give us a share; with your love
inspire us; by your spirit guide us; by your power protect us;
in your mercy receive us, now and always. Amen.

*(From an ancient collect)*

\* \* \*

*Reflections*

The sin of one person harms other people just as one person's holiness helps another.

*(Pope Paul VI)*

The one who endures to the end will be saved.

*(Matthew 24:13)*

A thousand offences which we truly acknowledge and confess ourselves to be guilty of, are not as perilous or damag-
ing as a single offence which we do not, or will not, recognise and acknowledge.

*(John Tauler)*

**Revere the Lord**

Revere the Lord, you his saints; they lack nothing, those who
  revere him.

Strong lions suffer and go hungry, but those who seek the
  Lord lack no blessing.

Come, children, and hear me that I may teach you to revere
  the Lord.

Who are they who long for life, and many days to enjoy their
  prosperity?

Then keep your tongue from evil, and your lips from
  speaking deceit.

Turn aside from evil and do good; seek and strive after
  peace.

*(Adapted from Psalm 33:10-15)*

**Thanks to the Suffering Servant of God**

Our Lord and Saviour: you endured the suffering and pain
  that should have been ours.

Our Lord and Saviour, we thank you.

We are healed by the punishments you suffered, made
  whole by the blows you received.

Our Lord and Saviour, we thank you.

You were treated harshly but endured it humbly; you never
  said a word.

Our Lord and Saviour, we thank you.

You were arrested and sentenced and led off to die, and no
  one cared about your fate.

Our Lord and Saviour, we thank you.

It was the Father's will that you should suffer; your death
  was a sacrifice to bring us forgiveness.

Our Lord and Saviour, we thank you.

You willingly gave your life and shared the fate of sinners.

Our Lord and Saviour, we thank you.

You took the place of many sinners and prayed that they
  might be forgiven.

Our Lord and Saviour, we thank you.

*(Adapted from Isaiah 53:4, 5, 7, 8, 10, 12)*

**For those who suffer**

Be merciful, Lord, to all our sisters and brothers who suffer any kind of persecution or affliction, whether in mind or body, and especially those who suffer for your name and gospel; give them patience, constancy and steadfast hope until you send them full and generous deliverance from all their troubles; through Christ our Lord. Amen.

*(Adapted from Christian Prayers, 1566 AD)*

**A lively, active and cheerful spirit**

Deliver me, Lord God, from a lazy mind, from half-heartedness and self-pity. I know these cannot but deaden my love for you. Mercifully free my heart from them, and give me instead a lively, active and cheerful spirit so that I may vigorously perform what you command, thankfully suffer whatever you choose for me, and be willing to obey in all things your holy love. Amen.

*(Adapted from John Wesley)*

\* \* \*

*Reflections*

Constancy in prayer becomes a habit, which then turns into a natural state.

*(Hesychius)*

None are so rich that they do not need another's help; none are so poor as not to be useful in some way to their fellow human beings.

*(Pope Leo XIII, Graves de Communi)*

All who want to live a godly life in Christ Jesus will be persecuted.

*(2 Timothy 3:12)*

### Seeking and finding

Lord our God, grant us grace to desire you with our whole heart so that, by so desiring, we may seek you and find you; and so finding you we may love you; and loving you we may hate those sins from which you have redeemed us. We ask this for the sake of Jesus Christ. Amen.

*(Adapted from Saint Anselm)*

### Thank you, Lord

Thank you, Lord, for the week that has passed. Thank you too for your love and protection.

Forgive me for any wrong I have done this week: if I have been bad-tempered or hard to live with; if I have hurt those I should love; for any word of comfort, praise or thanks which I might have spoken and did not speak; for any help I might have given to someone in need and did not give.

Lord, I pray tonight for all men and women: for the believer and the unbeliever; for those who are trying to find you and for those who are trying to ignore you.

Bless those who are lonely and who feel their loneliness most of all in the evening.

Bless those who are sick or old or who will not sleep tonight. Bless all homes and families and those who have no home of their own.

Give everyone restful sleep and the peace of heart that comes from knowing that our sins are forgiven and that we are always in the hands of our heavenly Father. Amen.

*(Adapted from the Irish Redemptorists)*

### Those who have gone before us

Grant, Lord, that we may remember gladly and gratefully those who have gone before us, who have stood by us and helped us in past days, cheered us by their sympathy and strengthened us by their example. And when the time comes for us to leave this world may we have a good hope of rest with them in paradise, through him in whose life we live, Jesus Christ our Saviour and Redeemer. Amen.

*(Adapted from the Church of Ireland)*

## Keep watch, Lord

Keep watch, Lord, with those who wake, or watch, or weep this night, and give your angels charge over those who sleep. Tend the sick, give rest to the weary, sustain the dying, calm the suffering, and pity the distressed; all for your love's sake, Christ our Redeemer. Amen.

*(Adapted from the Society of Saint Francis)*

## Blessing

May the blessing of almighty God, the Father, the Son and the Holy Spirit come down upon us and remain with us forever. Amen.

*(Adapted from the Roman liturgy)*

\* \* \*

*Reflections*

Every day call this prayer to mind, and repeat it to yourself as often as possible: 'Lord, have mercy on all who appear before you today.' For at every hour and every moment thousands of people depart from this earthly life and their souls appear before God – and how many of them depart in loneliness, unknown to anyone, sad and dejected because no one feels sorrow for them or even cares whether they are alive or not! And then, perhaps, from the other end of the earth your prayer for the repose of their souls will rise up before God, although you never knew them nor they you. How deeply moving it must be, as people stand in fear and trembling before the Lord, to know that at that very instant there is someone to pray even for them, that there is a fellow creature on earth who loves them! And God will look on both of you more favourably, for if you have had so much pity on them, how much greater will God's pity be, for God is infinitely more loving and merciful than you! And he will forgive them for your sake.

*(Fyodor Dostoyevsky)*

Lord Jesus, receive my spirit.

*(Acts 7:59)*

**Holy Virgin Mary**

Holy Virgin Mary, you are the joy of my soul. You are the dew of heaven to relieve my parching thirst. You are the stream of God's grace, flowing out from his heart into mine. You are the light of my darkened soul. You are the healing of my wounds.

You are the strength of my weakness. You are the consolation of my hardship.

You are the easing of my trouble. You are the loosing of my chains. You are the help of my salvation. Hear me, I beg you, virgin most faithful, take pity on me. Do not turn away from my need. Let my tears move you. Let your own compassionate heart move you. I cry to you, Mother of God and lover of the human race.

Hear me, poor sinner that I am, and grant me the grace I ask of you, Mary my Mother.

*(Celtic)*


**The reward of the just**

Happy are those who revere the Lord, who greatly delight in his commands.

Their descendants will be mighty in the land; the generation
    of the upright will be blessed.

Wealth and riches are in their houses, and their justice
    endures forever.
They are a light in the darkness for the upright; they are
    generous, merciful and just.

The good take pity and lend; they conduct their affairs with
    honour.
The just will never waver; they will be remembered for ever.

They have no fear of evil news; with a firm heart they trust
    in God.
With a steadfast heart they will not fear; they will see the
    downfall of evil.

Open-handed they give to the poor; their justice stands firm
    for ever.
Their heads will be raised in honour.

*(Adapted from Psalm 111)*

**Never-failing providence**
Lord God, whose never-failing providence orders all things both in heaven and on earth, we ask you to put away from us all harmful things and to give us those things that are of benefit to us, through Christ our Lord. Amen.

*(Adapted from the Society of Saint Francis)*

**May the blessed Virgin Mary protect us**
May the blessed Virgin Mary protect us.
Through her, God has given us the author of life, Jesus Christ our Lord. Amen.

*(Pope Paul VI)*

\* \* \*

*Reflections*

In Mary the church joyfully contemplates that which she herself desires and hopes wholly to be.

*(Vatican II, from Sacrosanctum Concilium)*

There is more hope for fools than for those wise in their own eyes.

*(From Proverbs 26:12)*

My will was perverse and lust had grown from it, and when I gave in to lust habit was born, and when I did not resist the habit it became a necessity.

*(Saint Augustine)*

### Jesus Christ, I want you, you want me

Jesus Christ, I want you for my own sake because I am so weak, I am a sinner. I want you for your sake so that I may know you, love you and become like you. I want you for the sake of others that I may do them no harm but rather good, so that I may give you to them.

Jesus Christ, you want me for my own sake, because you made me, you died for me, you love me. You want me for your sake that I may be your joy, your crown and be one with you. You want me for the sake of others so that through me you may help others, teach others and give yourself to others.

Jesus Christ, you shall have me, all that I have, all that I am, all that I possibly can be, for ever and ever. Amen.

*(Adapted from Alban Goodier)*


### Let me rely on you

Jesus, it is easy to be discouraged when I strive for holiness but don't seem to get very far. Let me rely on you and not on my own feeble powers. Your life seemed a failure but you went on loving us to the end, and that is the way you want us to love one another. You know my weakness and my sinfulness; heal the depths I cannot reach, and transform my violence into gentleness, my fear into confidence, my anger into patient love. Lord Jesus Christ, set me in your radiance; fill me with your Spirit and purify my heart. Amen.

*(Elizabeth Ruth Obbard)*


### Come with power into my soul

I ask you, gentle Mary, give me strength of mind, enlighten my thoughts, keep me chaste, sanctify my emotions, and make me truly large-hearted and single-minded. Come with power into my soul to give light to my conscience. May your strength and your grace safeguard me in temptation, console me in my trials, protect me in danger, and ever keep me from sin. Amen.

*(Saint Ildefonsus)*

**The sword of your Spirit**

God, whose word is sharper than a two-edged sword, piercing both heart and conscience deeply, let the sword of your Spirit pierce us through, and grant that the wounds which are made by your truth may be healed by your love; through Christ our Lord. Amen.

*(Adapted from the Church of Ireland)*

**Watch over us**

Watch over us, Lord, this night. By your strength may we rise at daybreak to rejoice in the resurrection of Christ your Son, who lives and reigns for ever and ever. Amen.

*(Adapted from the Roman liturgy)*

**Blessing**

May Christ our true God, at the prayers of his Mother and of the saints who bore God in their hearts, have mercy on us and save us, for he is gracious and loves all people. Amen.

*(Adapted from the Orthodox)*

\* \* \*

*Reflections*

The word of God is living and active, sharper than any two-edged sword, piercing until it divides soul from spirit, joints from marrow; it is able to judge the thoughts and intentions of the heart.

*(Hebrews 4:12)*

At the end of life, I will not be concerned about the mistakes I've made, or even the sins I've committed, but how unaware I was of how God loved me.

*(Enda Heffernan)*

Feed your mind daily with holy scripture.

*(Saint Jerome)*

## We praise and glorify you

God our Father, we praise and glorify you. You are the creator and Lord of all. We thank you for the gifts of life, faith, hope and love. Give a new outpouring of your Spirit to your people. Awaken in our hearts the gifts we received in baptism. Unite us in love and give us peace. Grant this in Jesus' name. Amen.

*(Anon)*

## What is yours

Lord Jesus, acknowledge what is yours in us, and take away from us all that is not yours; for your honour and glory. Amen.

*(Saint Bernardine of Siena)*

## You are the bread of life

Christ, Master and God, King of the ages, Maker of all things, I thank you for the gifts you have given me, and especially for the gift of sharing in your pure and life-giving mysteries. Therefore, I ask you, gracious Lord who loves all people, to preserve me under your protection and beneath the shadow of your wings. Grant me to the very end of my life to share worthily and with a clean conscience in your holy things, for the remission of sins and unto eternal life. For you are the bread of life, the fountain of all holiness, the giver of all good; and to you we give glory with the Father and the Holy Spirit, now and for ever, to the ages of ages. Amen.

*(Adapted from Saint Basil)*

## Pastors and people

Grant, Lord, that your people may have true affection for their pastors, and receive in turn their loving care. And so that both may persevere to the end, grant them unfailing loyalty and a sense of justice. Amen.

*(Adapted from the Leonine Sacramentary)*

**Be with this household**

God, protector of the faithful and constant companion of those who obey you, be with all the people who live in this house, so that while we care for them with human love, you may protect them with your divine power. Grant this for your love's sake. Amen.

*(Adapted from the Gelasian Sacramentary)*

**Receive these offerings**

Holy Trinity, receive these offerings which I, a sinner, offer both for myself and for the whole Christian people, for our sisters and brothers and for those who remember us regularly in their prayers, so that in this present world we may deserve to receive forgiveness of all our sins, and in the next deserve to attain to eternal rest, through Jesus Christ, the Redeemer of the world, who with the Father and the Holy Spirit lives and reigns for ever and ever. Amen.

*(Anon, eleventh century)*

\* \* \*

*Reflections*

Blessed are those who are persecuted for righteousness' sake, for theirs is the kingdom of heaven.

*(Matthew 5:10)*

In the sacrament of the Eucharistic bread, the unity of believers, who form one body in Christ, is both expressed and brought about.

*(Vatican II, Lumen Gentium)*

The Christian family is rightly called the living cell of the church.

*(Pope Paul VI, Matrimonia Mixta)*

### That I may learn to pray

God the creator of the universe, grant that I may learn to pray; grant that I may become worthy of being heard by you; grant that in the end I may be set free by you.

*(Adapted from Saint Augustine)*

### Your word of life

Lord God, your word of life gives us a new birth. May we receive it with open hearts, live it with joy, and express it in love. We ask this in the name of Jesus Chirst our Lord and loving Saviour. Amen.

*(Adapted from the Roman liturgy)*

### Glory to God our Saviour

To him who is able to keep us from falling, and to make us stand without blemish in the presence of his glory with rejoicing, to the only God our Saviour, through Jesus Christ our Lord, be glory, majesty, might and authority, before all time and now, and forever. Amen.

*(Adapted from Jude 24, 25)*

### For the church

Lord God, you named your church as your spouse. As it becomes graceful in your sight by devoted and trusting faith, so may it always have a lover's loyalty. Grant that all peoples honouring your name may be worthy of the Christian title they bear. May all in your church, closely united to you, revere you, love you, and follow you, so that walking always in your footsteps and under your guidance, we may deserve to attain the heavenly kingdom of your promise. Amen.

*(Adapted from Abbot Grimald)*

### For pastors

With minds humbled before you, eternal God, we earnestly pray that your friends, the pastors whom you have joined by a sacred bond, may always and with all their hearts be wholly obedient to you. By the intercession of blessed Peter your apostle, may they be filled with the spirit of charity, be freed from all passion for earthly things and worthy of your gifts of eternal joy.

*(Adapted from the Missal of Robert of Jumièges)*

**Help young people**

Spirit of holiness, who pour out your gifts on all believers and especially on those called to be Christ's ministers, help young people to discover the beauty of the divine call. Teach them the way of prayer, which is nourished by the word of God. Help them to read the signs of the times, so as to be faithful interpreters of your gospel and bearers of salvation. In the name of Jesus Christ, our Lord and loving Saviour. Amen.

*(Adapted from Pope John Paul II)*

**Blessing**

Lord God, may we live in awe of you, die in your grace, rest in your peace, rise in your power, and reign in your glory; for the sake of your son, Jesus Christ our Lord. Amen.

*(Adapted from Archbishop Laud)*

\* \* \*

*Reflections*

Prayer always remains the voice of those who apparently have no voice.

*(Pope John Paul II, Dominum et Vivificantem)*

Although the church is diverse in the multiplicity of her members, she is nevertheless welded into one by the fire of the Holy Spirit. If she seems divided into parts across bodily space, the sacrament of her interior unity is nonetheless too strong for her own integrity to be disrupted.

*(Saint Peter Damian)*

The servants [of God] will worship him; they will see his face, and his name will be on their foreheads. And there will be no more night; they need no light of lamp or sun, for the Lord God will be their light, and they will reign forever and ever.

*(Adapted from Revelation 22:3-5)*

**Enter my soul**
Let me know you, my Father, let me know you as I am
known by you. Enter my soul, you who are its strength, and
make it what you want.

*(Adapted from Saint Augustine)*

**I honour you**
God, almighty, all-knowing, supreme and infinite Good,
Wisdom above all wisdom, Life and Light of creatures, I
magnify and honour you.

*(Adapted from Gilbert Shaw)*

**May I be made strong**
Gracious Father, fill me with the knowledge of your will, in
all spiritual wisdom and understanding. Then I will be able
to live a life worthy of the Lord, fully pleasing to him, bearing fruit in every good work, as I grow in the knowledge of
God. May I be made strong with all the strength that comes
from his glorious power, and may I be prepared to endure
everything with patience, while joyfully giving thanks to
you, Father, who have enabled me to share in the inheritance
of the saints in light. You have rescued me from the power of
darkness and transferred me into the kingdom of your
beloved Son, in whom I have redemption, the forgiveness of
sins.

*(Adapted from Colossians 1:9-14)*

**Gladness and peace**
Grant us, Lord, to spend this day in gladness and peace,
without stumbling and without stain, so that reaching the
evening victorious over all temptation, we may praise you,
the eternal God, who are blessed, and govern all things to
the end of the age. Amen.

*(Mozarabic liturgy)*

**Obtain what you graciously promised**
God of mercy and pity, grant us such grace that we, by following your commandments, may obtain what you graciously promised and share in your life in heaven; through
Jesus Christ our Lord. Amen.

*(From the Gelasian Sacramentary)*

**For our friends**

Blessed Lord and Saviour, who has commanded us to love one another, grant us grace that, having received your undeserved generosity, we may love everyone in you and for you. We ask your blessing on all, but especially on the friends whom your love has given us. May you love them, fountain of love, and make them to love you with all their heart, with all their mind, and with all their soul that they may will, and speak, and do, only those things which are pleasing to you. Although our prayer is cold because our charity has so little fervour, yet you are rich in mercy. Do not measure out your goodness to them according to the dullness of our devotion, but as your kindness surpasses all human affection, so let your hearing transcend our prayer. Do to them what is good for them, according to your will, so that they, being always and everywhere ruled and protected by you, may attain in the end to everlasting life. And to you, with the Father and the Holy Spirit, be all honour and praise for ever and ever. Amen.

*(Saint Anselm)*

\* \* \*

*Reflections*

Then Mary said, 'Here am I, the servant of the Lord; let it be done with me according to your word.'

*(Luke 1:38)*

All of us know what it is to be tired, exhausted, grey with weariness, and at those times too we must allow ourselves, without strain, just to be like that, in the presence of God.

*(Wendy Robinson)*

With the Lord one day is like a thousand years, and a thousand years are like one day.

*(2 Peter 3:8)*

**Blessed be God**

Blessed be God who lives forever,
because his kingdom lasts throughout all ages.
Exalt him in the presence of every living being,
because he is our Lord and he is our God;
he is our Father and he is God forever.
He will afflict you for your iniquities,
but he will again show mercy on all of you.
If you turn to him with all your heart and all your soul,
to do what is true before him,
then he will turn to you
and will no longer hide his face from you.
So now see what he has done for you;
acknowledge him at the top of your voice.
Bless the Lord of righteousness, and exalt the King of the
ages.

*(Adapted from Tobit 13:1, 4-6)*

**According to conscience**

Since you, God, are supreme wisdom and have also made us
human beings to be gifted with intelligence, it is certain that
we cease to have part with you insofar as we stray from the
path of justice, and that we remain like you insofar as we do
not abandon the law of truth and sincerity. We ask you, then,
God of heavenly power that, scorning the shifty ways of
insincerity, we may follow what is according to our conscience and vocation. Grant this in Jesus' name. Amen.

*(Leonine Sacramentary)*

**Forgive us**

Forgive us, Father in heaven, for any wrong we have
thought or spoken or done this day. Give us strength to fight
more bravely tomorrow against our sins. Bless all whom we
love, and keep them safe this night, for the sake of Jesus our
Saviour. Amen.

*(Anon)*

**Blessing**

Bless us, God the Father who created us.
Bless us, God the Son who redeemed us.
Bless us, God the Holy Spirit who sanctifies us.
Blessed Trinity, keep us in body, soul and spirit unto ever-lasting   life. Amen.

*(Weimarischer Gesangbuch)*

\* \* \*

*Reflections*

Seek good and not evil, that you may live; and so the Lord, the God of hosts, will be with you. Hate evil and love good, and establish justice.

*(Adapted from Amos 5:14-15)*

The person who prays will have a heart as wide as the love of God itself.

*(Mother Mary Clare)*

Our task is not to claim, and name, and number … but to ponder and to wonder.

*(Jerry Harry Hellman)*

### The graces of the Holy Spirit

Merciful God, we ask you to fill our hearts with the graces of the Holy Spirit, with love, joy, peace, longsuffering, gentleness, goodness, faith, meekness and temperance. Teach us to love those who hate us, and to pray for those who treat us with contempt, so that we may be the children of you, our Father, who make the sun shine on the evil and the good, and the rain to fall on unjust and just alike. In hard times grant us to be patient; in good times keep us humble; may we guard our lips; may we treat lightly the pleasures of this world and thirst after those of eternity; through Jesus Christ our Lord. Amen.

*(Adapted from Saint Anselm)*

### Lord, my God

Lord, my God, you are the only Lord! I love you with all my heart, with all my soul and with all my strength. Help me to show how much I love you by loving my neighbour as I love myself.

*(Adapted from Mark 12:28-34)*

### Father, we thank you

Father in heaven, we give thanks for life and the experiences life brings. We thank you for our joys, sorrows, trials, failures and triumphs. Above all we thank you for the hope we have in Christ that we shall find fulfilment in him.

We praise you for our country, its beauty, the riches it has for us and the gifts it showers on us. We thank you for your peoples, the languages they speak, their variety of race, their cultural inheritance and the possibilities for greatness that lie in them. Grant that we accept these gifts with thankfulness and use them for the good of the human race and so bring glory to you; through Jesus Christ our Lord. Amen.

*(Anon, from India)*

### Our life in reverence and obedience

Grant, Lord, that all the days of our life may be so spent in reverence and obedience to you that we may together end

our lives in the praise and glory of your name; through Jesus
Christ our Lord. Amen.

*(Adapted from the Church of Scotland)*

**Shine in our hearts**
Shine in our hearts, loving Master, by the pure light of
knowledge of yourself, and open the eyes of our mind to the
contemplation of your teaching, and put into us reverence
for your blessed commandments. Setting aside all that is
hostile to you, may we follow a spiritual path, thinking and
doing all things according to your good pleasure.
For you are our sanctification and our illumination, and to
you we give glory, Father, Son and Holy Spirit, now and
ever, and to the ages of ages. Amen.

*(Adapted from the Orthodox)*

\* \* \*

*Reflections*

Everywhere, no matter where you find yourself, you can
erect an altar to God in your heart by means of prayer.

*(Saint John Chrysostom)*

The unity of all divided humanity is the will of God.

*(Pope John Paul II, Ut Unum Sint)*

But I say to you that listen, 'Love your enemies, do good to
those who hate you, bless those who curse you, pray for
those who abuse you.'

*(Luke 6:27)*

**As night closes in**
As night closes in, Lord, we give you thanks for the day that has run its course and we pray that tomorrow may see us safe and giving you praise and thanks.

*(Adapted from the Missal of Robert of Jumièges)*

**The gift of the Holy Spirit**
Lord, who bestowed the gift of the Holy Spirit on the apostles while they were at prayer, grant us a share in that same gift; through Christ our Lord. Amen.

*(Adapted from the Roman liturgy)*

**We praise and thank you**
God, your love is beyond measure and your blessings cannot be counted; we praise and thank you for all your goodness, you who are our strength in weakness, our light in darkness and our comfort in sorrow. From everlasting to everlasting you are God, Father, Son and Holy Spirit. Amen.

*(Adapted from the Church of Ireland)*

**Remember me, my God**
Remember me, my God, according to the greatness of your steadfast love.

*(Adapted from Nehemiah 13:22)*

**Grant us insight**
May the Lord grant us insight into the great mysteries of his kingdom, even as he has granted us knowledge of his holy word. As he has placed the seeds of truth in our minds, so may he by that truth protect us in temptation. Then his generous gift of grace will bear fruit in us even to a hundredfold.

*(Adapted from the Benedictional of Robert of Jumièges)*

**Father, Son and Holy Spirit**
I am bending my knee in the eye of the Father who created me, in the eye of the Son who purchased me, in the eye of the Spirit who cleansed me, in friendship and affection.

Holy God, through your own Anointed One, bestow on us fullness in our need: love towards God, the affection of God, the smile of God, the grace of God, reverence for God, and the will of God to do in the world as the angels and saints do in heaven.

Each shade and light, each day and night, each time in kindness, give us your Spirit. Amen.

*(Celtic)*

**Blessing**
May the Lord Jesus Christ fill us with tranquil joy, may his Spirit make us strong and tranquil in the truth of his promises. And may the blessing of the Lord come upon us abundantly. Amen.

*(Anon)*

\* \* \*

*Reflections*

You are my lamp, Lord; the Lord lightens my darkness.
*(Adapted from 2 Samuel 22:29)*

When comparing doctrines with one another, it should be remembered that in Catholic doctrine there exists an order or 'hierarchy' of truths, since they vary in their relation to the foundation of the Christian faith.
*(Vatican II, Unitatis Redintegratio)*

Inasmuch as you hate your brother or sister, it is God whom you hate.

*(Abbot Pachomius)*

### Faithfully to love you

God of strength, surpassing all understanding, who mercifully gives to your people both mercy and judgment, grant
to us, we ask you, faithfully to love you, and to walk this day
in the path of righteousness; through Jesus Christ our Lord.
Amen.

*(Adapted from the Sarum Breviary)*


### Blest is God

Blest is God who desires that all should be saved and come
    to the knowledge of the truth.
Blest is God who gives light and sanctification to everyone
    who comes into the world.
Blest are they whose sins are forgiven and wiped away.
Blest are they to whom the Lord imputes no wrong and in
    whose mouth is no deceit.
Christ our God, rich in mercy, who clothe yourself in light,
    grant me to be radiant with light.

*(Adapted from Orthodox baptismal liturgy)*


### May we welcome all truth

Grant, God, that we may wait patiently so as to know your
will. May we welcome all truth, under whatever form it
may be spoken. May we bless every good deed, no matter
who does it. May we rise above all strife to the contemplation of your eternal truth and goodness; through Jesus
Christ our Saviour. Amen.

*(Attributed to Charles Kingsley)*


### The Lord is my shepherd

The Lord is my shepherd, there is nothing I shall want.
Fresh and green are the pastures where he gives me repose.
Near restful waters he leads me, to revive my drooping spir-
it.

He guides me along the right path; he is true to his name.
If I should walk in the valley of darkness, no evil would I
    fear.
You are there with your crook and staff; with these you give
    me comfort.

You have prepared a banquet for me in the sight of my foes.
My head you have anointed with oil, my cup is overflowing.

Surely goodness and kindness shall follow me all the days of
    my life.
In the Lord's own house shall I dwell for ever and ever.

*(Psalm 22)*

\* \* \*

*Reflections*

Christians are not distinguished from the rest of humanity in
locality or speech or customs. But while they live in the cities
of the Greeks or the barbarians and follow local customs in
dress and food, yet the constitution of their own citizenship
is marvellous, and contradicts expectation. They live in their
countries, but only as travellers; they bear their share as cit-
izens and endure all hardships as strangers. Every foreign
country is their homeland, and every homeland is foreign to
them. They marry like others and have children; but they do
not expose their children to die. They have their meals in
common, but not their wives. They are in the flesh, but do
not live according to the flesh. Their existence is on earth,
their citizenship in heaven. They obey the laws and surpass
them in their lives. They love all people and are persecuted
by all. They are ignored and condemned, put to death and
endowed with life. They are beggars who make many rich,
in want of everything and abounding in everything. They
are dishonoured and in their dishonour glorified. They are
abused and vindicated. Reviled, they bless; insulted, they pay
their respects. They are punished for doing good, and rejoice
in this, as thereby stimulated to life. Those who hate them
cannot tell the reason for their hostility to them. In a word,
what the soul is to the body, this the Christians are in the
world.

*(From the anonymous second-century Epistle to Diognetus, 5)*

### Send your truth into our hearts

Almighty God, we ask and pray you, the fountain of ever-lasting light, to send your truth into our hearts and to pour upon us the glory of your brightness; through Christ our Lord. Amen.

*(Adapted from the Sarum Breviary)*

### The road I must travel

I call upon you, my God, my mercy, my creator. I had forgotten you, but you held me ever in your sight. Late have I loved you, beauty so ancient and so new, late have I loved you. Lord, heal and open my eyes that I may recognise your will. Show me the road I must travel so that I may see you.

*(Adapted from Saint Augustine)*

### By grace we have been saved through faith

God, rich in mercy, out of the great love with which you loved us, even when we were dead through our trespasses, you made us alive in Christ. By grace we have been saved through faith. You raised us up and seated us in the heavenly places in Christ Jesus. We are what you have made us, created in Christ Jesus for good works, which God prepared beforehand to be our way of life. How great you are!

*(Adapted from Ephesians 2:4-6, 8, 10)*

### Be patient with us sinners

We ask you, Lord our God, to be patient with us sinners. You who know our weakness, protect the work of your hands now and in the time to come. Deliver us from all temptation and danger, and from the power of evil in this world, and bring us to the kingdom of your only Son and our God.

For to your most holy Name be the glory, Father, Son and Holy Spirit, now and for ever, to the ages of ages. Amen.

*(Adapted from the Orthodox)*

### Teach me self-control

Teach me self-control by teaching me patience; teach me the knowledge of things by enlightening my understanding.

*(Prosper of Aquitaine)*

**Preserve us**
Most loving Father, you wish us to give thanks for all things, to fear nothing but the loss of you, and to cast all our care on you who care for us. Preserve us from faithless fears and worldly anxieties, and grant that no cloud of this mortal life may hide from us the light of that love which is immortal, and which you have revealed to us in your Son Jesus Christ. Amen.

*(Adapted from the Church of Ireland)*

**Blessing**
May God almighty bless us with his Holy Spirit.
May he guard us in our going out and our coming in.
May he keep us steadfast in his faith, free from sin and safe from all danger. Amen.

*(Anon)*

* * *

*Reflections*

God is love, and in the saints the Holy Spirit is love. Living in the Holy Spirit, the saints behold hell and embrace it, too, in their love.

*(Saint Silouan of Mount Athos)*

We proclaim Christ crucified, a stumbling block to Jews and foolishness to Gentiles, but to those who are the called, both Jews and Greeks, Christ is the power of God and the wisdom of God. For God's foolishness is wiser than human wisdom, and God's weakness is stronger than human strength.

*(Adapted from 1 Corinthians 1:23-25)*

Much of the frustration and stagnation in Christian circles today stems from a failure of imagination.

*(Ronald Rolheiser)*

**Ready to work**

A quiet night is your gift to us, Lord. Being alert in the morning and ready to work is also your gift. Give us to the full the enlightened mind that we desire, so that all the day long we may be refreshed in our soul with the power of your healing grace. Amen.

*(Bobbio Missal)*

**The unity which is your will**

Father, we pray for all Christians throughout the world: that they may share to the full in the work of your Son, revealing you to people and reconciling them to you and to one another; that they may learn to love one another and their neighbours as you have loved us; that they may more and more reflect the unity which is your will and your gift; we pray this through Christ our Lord. Amen.

*(Adapted from Coventry Cathedral prayer for unity)*

**Bless the Lord**

Bless the Lord, the great God!

Give thanks to the Lord of hosts, for the Lord is good, for his
     steadfast love endures forever!

Blessed be the glory of the Lord!

*(Adapted from Nehemiah 8:6; Jeremiah 33:11; Ezekiel 3:12)*

**Thank you for creatures**

God, I thank you for all the creatures you have made, so perfect in their kind: great animals like the elephant and the rhinoceros, funny animals like the camel and the monkey, friendly ones like the dog and the cat, working ones like the horse and the ox, timid ones like the squirrel and the rabbit, majestic ones like the lion and the tiger, and for birds with their songs. Lord, give us such love for your creation, that love may cast out fear, and all creatures see in us their priest and friend; through Jesus Christ our Lord. Amen.

*(Adapted from George Appleton)*

**For peace and unity**
Through the coming of the Holy Spirit, you, Christ our Lord, brought a deeper, more effective and lasting peace into the hearts of your disciples. We ask you to let our understanding of that peace drive personal animosity from our hearts. Because of our sins we are often deprived of true peace, but do you call us back to the happier atmosphere of Christlike concord, and bind us to each other with the firm bond of charity. Grant that we may live in unity, give us purity of body and soul and guide us to do your will. So, by this generously granted charity, may we be close friends with you. Amen.

*(Adapted from the Missale Mixtum)*

\* \* \*

*Reflections*

We wait for new heavens and a new earth, where righteousness is at home.

*(2 Peter 3:13)*

The deeper we delve into the harmonious disposition of the natural forces governed by eternal and unchangeable laws that are nevertheless hidden from our complete understanding, the more we feel ourselves moved to humble self-effacement, the more clearly we understand the range of our knowledge, the more eager becomes our effort to wrest further secrets from this inexhaustible fount of knowledge and power, and the more does our wonder grow in the presence of the infinite wisdom and order which permeates all creation.

*(Werner von Siemens)*

God, I want you, and I do not want anything else – this is the essence of pure contemplative prayer.

*(John Chapman)*

**Stay with us, Lord**
Stay with us, Lord, for it is towards evening and the day is far spent. Stay with us and with all your people. Stay with us in the evening of the day, in the evening of life and in the evening of the world. Stay with us and with all your faithful people, Lord, in time and in eternity. Amen.

*(Adapted from the Lutheran Manual of Prayer)*


**Teach us how to love**
Merciful Father, teach us how to love our enemies: to do good to those who hate us, to bless those who curse us and to pray for those who abuse us. May we give to everyone who begs from us. May we do to others as we would have them do to us.

*(Adapted from Luke 6:27-28; 30-31)*


**Praise and glory to the Trinity**
Praise and glory be to the power of the eternal Father who in his providence created the world out of nothing. Praise and glory be to the wisdom of his only-begotten Son who redeemed the world with his blood. Praise and glory be to the loving-kindness of the Holy Spirit who enlightened the world in faith. Praise and glory be to the holy and undivided Trinity who formed us in their image without our deserving it.

We give praise and glory to you, most blessed Trinity, for the blessing of our creation, by which you granted us bodies and souls. You adorned us with your image and likeness, and added us to your Christian people, making us sound and whole in our senses and in our members, above all the creatures who are beneath the heavens, and gave us your holy angels as our guides and servants. For all this be pleased that we may praise you, world without end. Amen.

*(Anon, eleventh century)*


**Confirm our hearts**
Merciful Lord, comforter and teacher of your faithful people, increase in us the desires you have given us, and confirm the hearts of those who hope in you by enabling us to

understand the depths of your promises, so that all your adopted children may even now see, with the eyes of faith, and patiently wait for, the light which as yet you do not openly reveal; through Jesus Christ our Lord. Amen.

*(Adapted from Saint Ambrose)*

**Blessing**

May the blessing of God almighty, the Father, the Son and the Holy Spirit rest upon us and upon all the work and worship done in his name.

May he give us light to guide us, courage to support us, and love to unite us, now and evermore. Amen.

*(Anon)*

\* \* \*

*Reflections*

God called to Moses out of the bush, 'Moses, Moses!' And he said, 'Here I am.' Then God said, 'Come no closer! Remove the sandals from your feet, for the place on which you are standing is holy ground.' God said further, 'I am the God of your father, the God of Abraham, the God of Isaac, and the God of Jacob.' And Moses hid his face, for he was afraid to look at God. Then the Lord said, 'I will send you to Pharaoh to bring my people, the Israelites, out of Egypt.' But Moses said to God, 'Who am I that I should go to Pharaoh, and bring the Israelites out of Egypt?' God said, 'I will be with you; and this will be the sign for you that it is I who sent you: when you have brought the people out of Egypt, you shall worship God on this mountain.'

*(Adapted from Exodus 3:4-7, 10-12)*

God is doing the work within. And it is not remarkable that the soul does not see this, for our senses cannot perceive that which God works in the soul.

*(Saint John of the Cross)*

One of the great difficulties about learning to meditate is that it is so simple. In our society most people think that only very complex things are worthwhile.

*(John Main)*

**Sovereign Saviour**

My Lord, my God, my sovereign Saviour Jesus Christ, I ask you wholeheartedly to take me, a sinner, to your great mercy and grace. For I wish to love you with all my heart and mind and with all my might, nor do I wish to love anything so much, either on or above the earth, save my Lord Jesus Christ. And insofar as I have until now failed to love and worship you above all things as my Lord, my God and my Saviour, Christ Jesus, I now ask you with a humble and a contrite heart to forgive my long neglect of the great love you have shown me when you offered your all-glorious body, God and man, to be crucified there on the cross. And remembering this firmly in my heart, I do not doubt, my Saviour Jesus Christ, that you will be near to me with your glorious presence, comforting me in body and soul, and at the last you will bring me to your everlasting joy which will have no end.

*(Adapted from a Processional of the nuns of Chester, fifteenth century)*

**Stand fast for truth and justice**

Almighty God, whose Son, our Lord and Saviour Jesus Christ, was moved with compassion for all who had gone astray, and with indignation for all who had suffered wrong; fill our hearts with your love, that we may seek out the lost, have mercy on the fallen, and stand fast for truth and justice; through Christ our Lord. Amen.

*(From Society of Saint Francis)*

**Those who suffer**

We remember, Lord, those who suffer from any kind of discrimination: your children, our brothers and sisters, who are humiliated and oppressed. We pray for those who are denied their human rights, for those unjustly imprisoned, and especially those who are tortured. Our thoughts rest a few moments with them *(pause)*; and we pray that your love and compassion may sustain them always. Amen.

*(Anon)*

**Your gracious promises**
Lord God who show your great power principally by mercy and forgiveness, grant to us such a measure of your grace that we, walking always in the way of your commandments, may obtain your gracious promises, and be made partakers of your heavenly blessings; through Jesus Christ our Lord. Amen.

*(Adapted from the Gelasian Sacramentary)*

**Bring me home again**
I am the lost sheep, wandering in the desert. Look out for me, Good Shepherd; bring me home again to your fold. Do with me as you will so that I may live with you all the days of my life and praise you for all eternity with all those who are with you in heaven. Amen.

*(Saint Jerome)*

\* \* \*

*Reflections*

If any want to become my followers, let them deny themselves and take up their cross and follow me.

*(Matthew 16:24)*

Anyone who rejects God's will is like a leaking ship on a stormy sea, is like an eagle caught in a trap, is like an apple tree which never blossoms.
Anyone who obeys God's will is like the golden rays of the summer sun, is like a silver chalice overflowing with wine, is like a beautiful bride ready for love.

*(Celtic)*

They would be very ignorant who would think that because enjoyment and delight [in prayer] are failing them, God is failing them, or who would think that, in having those, they are having God.

*(Saint John of the Cross)*

**Lift our hearts**
Almighty and everlasting God, you have put into our hearts
a longing for eternity and desires which the world cannot
satisfy. Lift our hearts, we ask you, above the narrow con-
fines of this present world to those of the world to come,
where you have prepared for us an inheritance that will
never fade away. We ask this through Christ our Lord.
Amen.

*(Adapted from the Church of Ireland)*

**Blessing and glory!**
The kingdom of the world has become the kingdom of our
Lord and of his Christ, and he will reign forever and ever!
Salvation and glory and power to our God, for his judg-
ments are true and just!
Blessing and glory and wisdom and thanksgiving and hon-
our and power and might be to our God forever and ever.
Amen.

*(Adapted from Revelation 11:15; 19:1-2; 7:12 )*

**Be with us all**
Comforting One, compassionate One, be with us all when
we suffer loss, and ache with the pain of grieving. Give us a
glimpse of the way it will be when love will never be taken
away, when life itself will not be diminished, when all that
we hold most precious will live and remain with us for ever.
Amen.

*(Miriam Thérèse Winter)*

**For one who has died**
With the souls of the faithful departed, give rest, Lord our
Saviour, to the soul of your servant *(name)*, preserving her
(him) unto the life of blessedness which is with you, Lover of
humanity.
In the place of your rest, Lord, where all your saints repose,
give rest also to the soul of your servant *(name)*, for you
alone love humanity.
Glory be to the Father and to the Son and to the Holy Spirit,
as it was in the beginning, is now, and ever shall be, world

without end. Amen.

You are the God who descended into hell and loosed the bonds of the captives. Do you also give rest to the soul of your servant *(name)*.

Virgin Mary, pure and undefiled, who, still a virgin, brought forth God, do you pray that her (his) soul may be saved.

With the saints give rest, Lord Christ, to the soul of your servant *(name)*, where there is neither sickness, nor sorrow, nor sighing but life everlasting.

*(Adapted from the Orthodox)*

**Blessing**

May the Lord lead us when we go, and keep us when we sleep and talk with us when we wake.

And may the peace of God which surpasses all understanding keep our hearts and our minds in Christ Jesus. Amen.

*(Anon)*

\* \* \*

*Reflections*

God is nearer to us than our own soul, for he is the ground in whom our soul stands.

*(Julian of Norwich)*

Pray in the Spirit at all times. Keep alert. Persevere in prayer.

*(From Ephesians 6:18)*

The line dividing good and evil cuts through the heart of every human being.

*(Alexander Solzhenitsyn)*

**Be with me, Lord**

Be with me, Lord, at my rising in the morning. Look kindly on me, Lord, and guide my actions, my words and my thoughts. Keep me in the right path so that I spend the day in accordance with your will. Give me reverence for you and a repentant heart. Guide my hearing that I pay no attention to backbiting, nor to untrue and foolish talk, but let me be alert for the voice of God. Watch my steps so that I do not go about idly from place to place but be united with the thought of God in my mind. Let me be of service to God this day with the work of my hands, and, in the evening, let me lift them up in prayer.

*(From the Book of Cerne)*

**Open to the Word**

Mary, virgin who listened, and virgin of the Word made flesh in your womb, help us to be open to the word of the Lord, so that, having been welcomed and meditated upon, it may grow in our hearts. Help us to live like you the beatitudes of believers and to dedicate ourselves with unceasing charity to bringing the Good News to all those who seek your Son. Grant that we may serve every person, becoming servants of the word we have heard, so that, remaining faithful to it, we may find happiness in living it. Amen.

*(Adapted from Pope John Paul II)*

**Cast away the works of darkness**

Almighty God, give us grace to cast away the works of darkness, and put on us the armour of light, now in this mortal life in which your Son Jesus Christ came to visit us with great humility, so that on the last day when he will come again in majesty to judge the living and the dead, we may rise to life eternal, through him who lives and reigns with you and the Holy Spirit, now and for ever. Amen.

*(Adapted from the Book of Common Prayer)*

**Heal me, Lord**

Heal me, Lord, and I shall be healed; save me and I shall be saved. You are the one I praise!

*(Adapted from Jeremiah 17:14)*

**Give grace, Father**
To all who live by the truths of the faith, give grace, Father,
that they may lead upright and holy lives, never departing
from your teaching. To those who have not yet found faith
in you, grant that before they leave this life they may come
to believe in you and to know the love of your holy name.
Then, having known it, may they keep it firm and inviolate.
Let the sacrifice of your body and blood win pardon for the
sins of the living and the dead. Amen.

*(Adapted from Anselm of Bury St Edmunds)*

\* \* \*

*Reflections*

What the Catholic faith believes about Mary is based on
what it believes about Christ, and what it teaches about
Mary illuminates in turn its faith in Christ.

*(Catechism of the Catholic Church)*

There is a danger of 'devout' people living for themselves
instead of living for others.

*(John Chapman)*

You do well if you really fulfil the royal law according to the
scripture, 'You shall love your neighbour as yourself.' But if
you show partiality, you commit sin and are convicted by
the law as transgressors.

*(James 2:8-9)*

## Give us yourself

Lord, give us yourself to be the light of our soul. Hear our prayers as we seek you, needing you, we who dare not trust in our own worth. For it is by your working in us that we fully live; it is by you that we are supported and by your grace that we are protected. Do not turn away, then, from those whose bond with you is so close, whose longing is for you, whose souls would cling to you and whose minds are ever set to follow you.

*(Spanish collect, seventh century)*

## Blessing of one's house

Blessed are you, Lord God, king of all creation: through your goodness you have given this house to be a home for us and for our family *(names)*. Let your peace remain with us always. Let all who come here to share our life find generosity, peace and happiness; may they depart enriched by the joy of Christian living. Blessed be God forever. Amen.

*(Adapted from the Roman Ritual)*

## You are worthy

You are worthy, our Lord and God, to receive glory and
    honour and power,
for you created all things, and by your will they existed and
    were created.

By your blood you ransomed us for God
from every tribe and language and people and nation.

You have made us to be a kingdom and priests serving our
    God,
and we will reign on earth.

Worthy is the Lamb that was slaughtered to receive power
    and wealth and wisdom
and might and honour, and glory and blessing!

*(Adapted from Revelation 4:11; 5:9, 10, 12)*

## I am heartily sorry for my sins

God, I am heartily sorry for having offended you, and I detest my sins because they offend you, Lord God, who are good and deserving of my love. I firmly resolve, with the help of your grace, to sin no more and to avoid the occasions of sin. Amen.

*(Anon)*

## Blessing

May the peace of God keep our hearts and minds in the knowledge and love of God, and of his Son Jesus Christ our Lord; and the blessing of God almighty, the Father, the Son and the Holy Spirit, be among us and remain with us always. Amen.

*(Adapted from the Book of Common Prayer)*

\* \* \*

*Reflections*

The family is the first school of work for every young person.

*(Pope John Paul II, Laborem Exercens)*

Your faith has made you well; go in peace.

*(Mark 5:34)*

We speak to God when we pray; we listen to him when we read the divine scriptures.

*(Saint Ambrose)*

# References and Acknowledgements

The author and publisher gratefully acknowledge the permission of the following to use their copyright material: Prayers Nos 168 and 180 from *A Book of Occasional Prayers* © The General Synod of the Church of Ireland, used with permission. Prayers Nos 22, 251, 228, 158, 310, 298, 160, 211, 235, 276, 77, 25, 304 and 291 from *A Book of Occasional Prayers* © The General Synod of the Church of Ireland adapted and used with permission; SPCK for prayers from *The SPCK Book of Christian Prayer, Praying with the Orthodox Tradition* and *The Wisdom of Saint Columba of Iona*; Continuum International Publishing Group for prayers from *Celebrating Common Prayer*; Darton, Longman and Todd for prayers from *Celtic Fire* edited by Robert van de Weyer; OUP for prayers from *The Oxford Book of Prayer* edited by George Appleton; St Anthony Messenger Press for prayers from *A Retreat with Thérèse of Lisieux: Loving our way into holiness* by E. R. Obbard ODC; Redemptorist Publications Dublin for prayers from *Come Lord Jesus: Redemptorist Mission and Novena Book*; Franciscan Press for prayers from *St Francis of Assisi: Writings and Early Biographies* edited by Marion A. Habig. Scripture quotations are from the *New Revised Standard Version*, copyright 1989 by the Division of Christian Education of the National Council of the Churches of Christ in the USA. Used by permission. (Some) Psalm texts are translated from the Hebrew by The Grail, © The Grail (England) 1963 and used by permission.

The following is a list of the principal sources consulted in the preparation of this book:

Appleton, George (ed.), *The Oxford Book of Prayer*, Oxford University Press, 1985.

Armstrong, Regis, *The Prayers of Saint Francis,* a leaflet, privately published.

Barclay, William, *Prayers for Young People* and *More Prayers for Young People,* St Pauls/BYB, Mumbai, India.

Boldoni, Valeria (comp.), *Praying with Augustine,* trans. by Paula Clifford, Triangle, London, 1997.

Bullen, Anthony and Brandley, James A., *Catholic Prayer Book,* Gweru, Zimbabwe, 1971.

Carmichael, Alexander (comp.), *Carmina Gadelica: Hymns and Incantations with Illustrative Notes and Words, Rites and Customs Dying and Obsolete,* Scottish Academic Press, Edinburgh, six vols., from 1900.

Church of Ireland, *A Book of Occasional Prayers,* Belfast, undated (probably about 1971).

Collins, William (comp. and ed.), *The Weekday Missal,* London, 1975.

Fox, Selina Fitzherbert, *A Chain of Prayer across the Ages: Forty Centuries of Prayer 2000 BC-AD 1955,* John Murray, London, 1956.

Habig, Marion A. (ed.), *St Francis of Assisi: Writings and Early Biographies,* English Omnibus edition, Franciscan Herald Press, Chicago, Illinois, USA, 1973.

Hurley, Dermot, *Everyday Prayerbook,* Chapman, London, 1979.

Law, Philip (comp.), *Praying with the Old Testament,* and *Praying with the New Testament,* Triangle, London, 1989.

McEvoy, Hubert (ed.), *Priestly Prayers,* Burns, Oates and Washbourne, London, 1961.

Murphy, Gerard (ed.), *Early Irish Lyrics, Eighth to Twelfth Century,* OUP, 1956.

Obbard ODC, Elizabeth Ruth, *A Retreat with Thérèse of Lisieux: Loving Our Way Into Holiness,* Saint Anthony Messenger Press, Cincinnati, Ohio, copyright 1996. Reprinted by permission of St. Anthony Messenger Press, 1615 Republic St., Cincinnati, OH 45210, USA. All rights reserved.

Ó Laoghaire, Diarmuid (ed.), *Our Mass, Our Life: some Irish traditions and prayers,* Messenger Publications, Dublin, 1968.

Parenti, Stefano (ed.), *Praying with the Orthodox Tradition*,
      trans. by Paula Clifford, Triangle, London, 1989.

Redemptorists, The Irish, *Come, Lord Jesus: Redemptorist
      Mission and Novena Book*, Dublin, no date.

Rotelle, John E. (ed.), *Tradition Day by Day: Readings from
      Church Writers*, Augustinian Press, Villanova,
      Pennsylvania, 1994.

Saint Vladimir's Seminary Press, *A Manual of Eastern
      Orthodox Prayers*, Crestwood, New York, 1983.

Shaw, Gilbert, *A Pilgrim's Book of Prayers*, SLG Press,
      Fairacres, Oxford, 1992.

Simpson, Ray (comp.), *Celtic Daily Light: A Spiritual Journey
      throughout the Year*, Hodder & Stoughton, London, 1997.

Society of Saint Francis, *Celebrating Common Prayer*,
      Mowbray, London, 1997.

SPCK, *The SPCK Book of Christian Prayer*, SPCK, London,
1996.

Talbot Press, Dublin, *Daily Prayer*, 1974.

Vatican Polyglot Press, *The Pope's Family Prayer Book*,
      Vatican City, 1975.

Watts, Murray (compiler), *The Wisdom of Saint Columba of
      Iona*, Past Times, Oxford, 1997.

Weyer, Robert van de (ed.), *Celtic Fire: an anthology of Celtic
      Christian Literature*, DLT, London, 1990.

Winstone, Harold (ed.), *The Sunday Missal*, Collins, London,
      1977.

# Index of Authors, Sources and Terms

*(In some cases, little or no information is available about contributors; therefore they are omitted. This is especially true of contemporary writers about whom there is no information in sources such as encyclopaediae or dictionaries of biography.)*

**Abélard, Peter** (1079-1142) Born near Nantes, France, he became canon and master of the cathedral school in 1115. He seduced Héloïse, one of his pupils, and was castrated in revenge by her uncle, Canon Fulbert, after which he became a monk. His writings on theology, and especially on logic, were controversial. He continued to teach but was charged with heresy and forced to retire. He ended his life as abbot of a monastery in Brittany.

**Alcuin** (735-804) Flaccus Albinus Alcuinus was born at York, England, where he became head of the cathedral school and established a library. In 782 Charlemagne called him to Aix-la-Chapelle to organise a school in the palace. In 796 he retired to the abbey of Saint Martin of Tours and founded a school there also. His writings include works on grammar, rhetoric, dialectic, astronomy, dogma, poetry, a revision of the Vulgate and a Missal. He is regarded as the virtual founder of education in the Frankish empire and the inspiration of the Carolingian renaissance.

**Alphonsus Liguori, Saint** (1696-1787) Born at Naples, Italy, he became a lawyer, then a priest in 1726. He founded the Redemptoristine nuns, and the Congregation of the Most Holy Redeemer (the Redemptorists) to preach the Christian faith to the people. His own speciality was moral theology where his outlook was gentle and liberal. In later life his relations with his own congregation were strained and he was removed from its leadership by Pope Pius VI. He was later made bishop and cardinal.

**Ambrose of Milan, Saint** (340-397) Born in Trier, Germany. Trained in law, he entered the civil service of the Roman Empire, becoming a provincial governor, residing in Milan. He was chosen by popular acclaim as the city's bishop, even though he was still unbaptised. After baptism and ordination, he gave his property to the poor and began an intensive study of scripture. He strongly opposed Arianism, a heresy which questioned the divinity of Christ. He had many conflicts with the Emperor Theodosius, insisting that a Christian emperor had to live like a Christian. He helped Saint Augustine in his difficulties with the Christian faith, and later baptised him. His feast is celebrated on 7 December.

**Andrewes, Lancelot** (1555-1626) A clergyman of the Church of England, he became bishop of Winchester in 1619, and was active in preparing the Authorised Version of the Bible. His sermons were noted for their intellectual and literary quality.

**Anselm of Bury St Edmund's** Anselm was abbot of this Benedictine monastery from 1121 to 1148. It was one of the most wealthy, powerful and influential monasteries in England for several centuries.

**Anselm of Canterbury, Saint** (1033-1109) Born in Aosta, Italy, he joined the Benedictines in France, becoming abbot at Le Bec before going to England where he was chosen to be archbishop of Canterbury. He struggled for the freedom of the church from royal control and was twice exiled. He also opposed the slave-trade. He wrote extensively on mystical theology of which his best-known is work is on the incarnation, *Cur Deus Homo?* His feast is on 21 April.

**Apostles' Creed** A statement of the essential articles of the Christian faith dating from a baptismal catechesis of the second or third century. It has no known connection with the apostles, and is so called because it is divided in twelve sections.

**Appleton, George** Began work as a curate of the Church of England in the east of London, then went as a missionary to Burma. After the Second World War, he returned to London, working at Saint Paul's Cathedral. He became archbishop of Perth in 1963, and archbishop in Jerusalem in 1969, retiring in 1974. He has published several books on prayer and spirituality.

**Augustine of Hippo, Saint** (354-430) Born at Thagaste in Tunisia, of a Christian mother, Monica, and a pagan father, Patricius, his early life was marked by his adherence to Manicheism and his sexual promiscuity. He was converted to the Christian faith at about the age of thirty two, and was baptised by Saint Ambrose of Milan in 387. He described this spiritual journey in *The Confessions*, perhaps the first autobiography ever written. Returning to Africa, he founded a semi-monastic community but, before long, he was chosen by popular acclamation and against his will to be bishop in the diocese of Hippo. Among his vast writings, one of the best-known is *On the City of God*, the first Christian philosophy of history, written to refute the charge that it was the conversion of Rome to Christianity which was bringing about its defeat by the barbarian tribes. Augustine died while Hippo was being besieged by the Vandals. His feast is celebrated on 28 August, the day after his mother, Saint Monica.

**Barclay, William** Ordained a minister in the Church of Scotland, he was professor of scripture at the University of Glasgow for many years since 1963. He wrote a commentary on the New Testament, and many other works, both popular and academic, in which he sought to bridge the gap between the academic world of theology and that of the plain person in the pew.

**Basil, Saint** (330-379) Born at Caesarea, Cappadocia, Turkey, he received an exceptional education. Though he would have preferred a quiet, retiring life he became bishop of Caesarea in 370. He was noted for his efforts against

Arianism, his concern for the poor, and for rehabilitating thieves and prostitutes. His writings are still widely read, especially those on the Holy Spirit and for monks, which are still followed by the Order of Saint Basil in the Eastern church. His feast is celebrated annually on 2 January.

**Bede, The Venerable** (673-735) Born at Wearmouth, England, he spent almost all his life at the monastery there and in Jarrow. Ordained priest by St John Beverley about 703 he wrote *The Ecclesiastical History of the English People*, in addition to homilies and 25 volumes of commentaries on scripture. His feast is celebrated on 25 May.

**Benedictional** A benedictional is a book of blessings or, more recently, one which contains the rite of Benediction of the Blessed Sacrament. The name derives from the Latin, *benedictio*, meaning a blessing.

**Beogna, Colmán Mac** (555-611) According to the *Annals of Ulster*, a disciple of Saint Colmcille, he founded a monastery at Lann Elo, near Durrow, Meath, Ireland, and wrote *The Alphabet of Devotion (Aibgítir in Chrábaid)*, probably based on the sayings of the same saint.

**Bernardine of Siena, Saint** (1380-1444) Born in Italy, he spent his teen years in caring for the sick during a plague. He later joined the Franciscans and became a priest. His outstanding life's work was his preaching on the name of Jesus. He fostered study and discipline in his order. His feast is celebrated on 20 May.

**Blue, Lionel** A Jewish rabbi who lives in England and contributes to the Catholic weekly, *The Tablet*.

**Bobbio Missal** A manuscript from the seventh century found by Jean Mabillon in the seventeenth century. It is an Irish document in Romanised form containing an Order of Mass for various days and intentions, the Order of Baptism, and a blessing of ashes. The manuscript is now in the

Bibliothèque Nationale in Paris. The monastery of Bobbio was founded by Saint Columbanus about the start of the seventh century.

**Bonaventure, Saint** (1218-1274) Born Giovanni di Fidanza at Bagnoregio in Tuscany, Italy, he joined the Franciscans in 1243 and studied in Paris, later becoming a teacher. He became Minister General of his Order at the age of 36 and had such influence that he has sometimes been called its second founder. His writings on philosophy and theology have left a lasting influence on the church; his theology is mystical more than dogmatic, affective more than rational. He died at Lyons, France, having succeeded at the general council of the church there in reconciling, albeit temporarily, the Eastern and Western churches. His feast is celebrated on 15 July.

**Book of Common Prayer.** See Common Prayer, Book of.

**Breviary** A book, or books, containing the *Divine Office*, said daily by priests, religious and some lay people. It is based on the psalms and other scripture readings, with hymns and prayers. A shorter version is published under the title *Daily Prayer*.

**Catechism of the Catholic Church.** A summarised statement of the teaching of the Catholic Church, published in 1997.

**Caussade, Jean-Pierre de** (? - 1751) Little is known of his early life, except that he joined the Jesuits at Toulouse, France, in 1693. He taught grammar at Auch and became rector of the college at Albi. His best-known work is *Self-Abandonment to Divine Providence*, and has been described as combining the depth and ardour of Saint John of the Cross with the warmth and humanity of Saint Francis de Sales.

**Celtic spirituality** There are strong links between pre-Christian and Christian Celtic spirituality: religion is a religion of nature, without a distinction between the sacred and the secular, nature and grace, and thus seeing all of life, even routine daily events and activities, as invested with religious significance. There was a profound sense of the immanence, or all-pervading presence, of God in life. John Scotus Eriugena was the great theologian of the Celtic world. His theology was inclusive, and it took creation rather than redemption as its starting point. In God, creating and being are one, so that the created world is itself a theophany, or manifestation of God. But Celtic spirituality was also transcendent with a sense of the majesty and wonder of God who is greater by far than his creatures. It is a gutsy, down-to-earth manly spirituality which is at home with sexuality. In the Christian world, the term 'Celtic' refers to Ireland, Scotland, Wales, the Isle of Man, Cornwall and Brittany, together with those parts of France, Germany, Switzerland and Italy where Saint Columbanus and his disciples founded monasteries. The Christian community took on board many of the ideas, attitudes and assumptions of pre-Christian Celtic tradition while seeking to remove elements which were incompatible with the Christian faith. The *Stowe Missal* and the *Carmina Gadelica* (six vols., Edinburgh, 1928) are outstanding examples of early and recent Celtic liturgy and spirituality.

**Cerne, Book of** A manuscript collection of prayers for private use, attributed to Aedelwald, a ninth century Saxon bishop attached to the Benedictine monastery of Cerne, Dorset, England. Now in the university library, Cambridge.

**Chapman, John** A Benedictine monk who lived at the start of the twentieth century, and served as a chaplain in the British army during the First World War. He corresponded widely on spiritual matters, and some of this correspondence has been published under the title of the *Spiritual Letters*.

**Chardin, Pierre Teilhard de** (1881-1955) Born at Sarcenet, in the Auvergne, France, he entered the Jesuits and trained in England. A palaeontologist by profession, he sought to present Christ as the focal point to which all creation leads. Influential among scientists, he was prohibited by the Holy Office from teaching or publishing any religious writings. He died in virtual exile in the United States. His writings such as *Le Milieu Divin, The Phenomenon of Man, Letters from a Traveller, Hymn of the Universe, The Future of Man* and *The Heart of Matter,* all published posthumously, have been widely influential.

**Chesterton, Gilbert Keith** (1874-1936) Born in London, England, he studied art before turning to journalism. His novels featuring Father Brown, a priest who solves crimes by drawing on his knowledge of human nature, are probably more popular than his works of controversy and apologetic.

**Chrysostom, Saint John** (349-407) Born in Antioch, Syria, he became bishop of Constantinople in 397. Famous for his preaching – the title 'Chrysostom' means 'of the golden mouth' – which vigorously denounced moral laxity, especially failure to help the poor while indulging in wasteful extravagance, he was twice exiled. Regarded as among the greatest of the saints of the Eastern churches, his feast is celebrated on 13 September.

**Church of Ireland** A constituent church of the Anglican communion, in Ireland; its primatial see is in Armagh. It was the Established church in Ireland until 1869.

**Collect** The opening prayer of the Mass, which 'collects' in one the prayers of the congregation.

**Colmcille** or **Columba, Saint** (c.521-597) Born in Gartan, Donegal, Ireland, and educated by Saint Finnian of Clonard, he founded monasteries in Durrow, Derry and elsewhere. In 563, he left Ireland for exile on the island of Iona off the west coast of Scotland from where he worked until his death for the conversion of the Picts. His influence on Celtic Christianity, especially on monastic life, was immense. The *Life of Saint Colm Cille* by Adamnán is of little historical value. The name Colmcille means 'dove of the church'; *Columba* is Latin for a dove. The saint's feast is celebrated on 9 June.

**Common Prayer, Book of** The official liturgical text for churches of the Anglican communion, it comprises in one volume a calendar, a lectionary, the rites of the Eucharist and the sacraments, the order of funerals, a profession of faith, and all rites needed for Anglican worship. The chief compiler was Thomas Cranmer, archbishop of Canterbury, who drew on the Sarum Missal, the medieval breviary, ritual and pontifical as well as elements from the Gallican and Greek liturgies. Its classical literary excellence has influenced not only Anglican worship but the development of the English language. The best-known editions are those of 1662 and 1928, though each self-governing church of the Anglican communion is free to devise its own text. It has been translated into about 150 languages.

**Cranmer, Thomas** (1489-1556) He became archbishop of Canterbury in 1533. In the same year he declared null and void the marriage of Henry VIII and Catherine of Aragon. Under Edward VI he was very influential in shaping the Church of England, forming its liturgy, drawing up the Thirty-nine Articles, and the prayer books of 1549 and 1552. When Mary Tudor, a Catholic, became queen he was condemned to death for heresy. Cranmer recanted but, when he realised that his life would not be spared, he resumed his former position and was burned at the stake, putting first into the flames the hand which had signed his recantation.

**Cyril of Jerusalem, Saint** (315-386) He became bishop of Jerusalem in 348. His involvement in the Arian controversy led to his being sent into exile three times for a total of sixteen years. His extant writings are mainly in the form of catechesis for catechumens and newly baptised. He was declared a doctor of the church in 1888; his feast is celebrated on 18 March.

**Decretals of Gratian.** See Gratian, Decretals of.

**Desert Fathers, The** In the Old Testament, the desert was sometimes seen as a place of seclusion for the purification and renewal of the community, a return to the sources, a stripping away of corruption and compromise. In Christian times, Saint Anthony of Egypt was seen as the first of those who left ordinary society to pursue the inner life. He was followed by others such as Pachomius who founded monastic settlements, and John Cassian who wrote his *Institutes* and *Conferences* for monks. The anecdotes and *Sayings of the Desert Fathers* date from the early fifth century. The Fathers have had a lasting influence on the church through the Benedictine Order, Charles de Foucauld and the retreat movement, among others.

**Dostoevsky, Fyodor** (1821-1881) Born in Moscow, Russia, the son of a doctor, he served for a time in the army. His writings, considered to be radical and socialist, caused him to fall foul of the tsarist authorities, who sentenced him to death. Reprieved, he served four years in a penal camp which had the effect of accentuating his epilepsy. His novels show profound spiritual and psychological insight, especially the discourses of Father Zossima in *The Brothers Karamazov*.

**Eckhart, Meister Johann** (about 1260-1327) Born at Hochheim in Germany, he joined the Dominican Order. A preacher, theologian and mystic, he used new language – speaking, for example, of God as female – in his theological writings. This involved him in difficulties with church leaders, even though his personal orthodoxy and morals were vindicated on examination. He taught theology in France and Germany and became the provincial of his Order in Saxony. He is regarded as the father of German mysticism.

**Epistle to Diognetus** An anonymously written apologetic in the form of a letter, from about the middle of the second century. Its theology has been described as sincere but vague, its style noble and elegant. Nothing is known of its origins, or of Diognetus.

**Ficino, Marsiglio** (1433-1499) An Italian, Ficino founded an academy in Florence in 1462 and became a priest in 1473. A philosopher, he created a synthesis of Platonism and medieval theology. He saw the human soul as having the central place in the universe and that it ascended to God through contemplation. His ideas on Platonic love became a popular theme of Renaissance literature.

**Francis de Sales, Saint** (1567-1623) Born at Anneçy, France, he studied law in Paris, then was ordained priest and became bishop of Geneva, Switzerland, in 1602. He worked hard for the education of clergy and faithful alike, insisting that the fulness of the Christian life was accessible to all. His two principal writings are *A Treatise on the Love of God* and *An Introduction to the Devout Life*, of which the latter was unique in its time in that it was written with laypeople particularly in mind. A renowned preacher, he worked with Saint Jane Frances Fremiot de Chantal for the foundation of the Visitation sisters. His feastday is on 24 January.

**Francis of Assisi, Saint** (1182-1226) Born John Bernardone in Assisi, Italy, and nicknamed Francis by his father, he enjoyed a carefree life of partying until taken prisoner in a local conflict. This helped to bring about a deeper commitment to God, following the gospel in simplicity and poverty. Followers gathered, and an order of brothers living in community according to the gospel was founded in 1209. Francis went to preach the gospel to the Sultan during a crusade, but without result. He encouraged Saint Clare of Assisi to found an order of nuns, while later he founded an order of lay men and women penitents, known today as the Secular Franciscan Order. Never ordained priest, he was, in 1224, the first known person to receive the stigmata of Christ in his body. His feast is celebrated on 4 October.

**Gallican liturgy** The liturgy in use in Gaul (France) between the fourth and eighth centuries. Not a systematic or comprehensive body of rites, its origins are uncertain. Romanised versions of it survive today in Toledo (see Mozarabic liturgy) and Milan.

**Gelasian Sacramentary** Dating from the mid-eighth century, and originating in the north-east of France, it has no connection with any Gelasius, that name being a later addition assigned by the eighteenth century Italian archivist, Lodovico Muratori. It probably is based on Roman and Gallican sources, now lost.

**Goodier, Alban M. R.** (1869-1939) Born in Great Harwood, Lancashire, England, he joined the Jesuits in 1887, was ordained priest in 1903, and bishop in 1919. He resigned as bishop in 1926 and took up writing. Among his better-known works are *The Public Life of our Lord Jesus Christ* (two vols.), 1930 and *The Passion and Death of Our Lord Jesus Christ*, 1933.

**Gratian, Decretals of** A collection of canonical decrees and extracts from the Fathers of the church and from Roman law made by John Gratian, a monk and professor at the university of Bologna about 1150. By it he sought to bring order into the mass of decrees issued by local church councils of both East and West.

**Gregorian Sacramentary** Beginning from Pope Saint Gregory I at the end of the sixth century, this Sacramentary went through a long and complex development, of which the principal parts were the work of Pope Adrian I, the *Hadrianum*, and additions by Alcuin, secretary to the Emperor Charlemagne. It continued in use until the eleventh century.

**Gregory Nazianzus, Saint** (c.329-390) Born at Nazianzus in Turkey, Gregory travelled widely as a young man, being educated in Palestine and Greece before undertaking a life of solitude. He was ordained priest and bishop against his will and refused to take up his appointment. However, the effectiveness of his preaching against Arianism led to his being appointed bishop of Constantinople in 380. His teaching on the divinity of Christ was accepted at the first Council of Constantinople in 381. Continuing internal church conflicts led to his return to Nazianzus where he died. His writings, especially on the Trinity and on Christ, led to his being given the name of 'The Theologian.' His feastday is on 2 January.

**Gregory of Nyssa, Saint** (c.330-c.395) Born in Caesarea, Cappadocia, Turkey, Gregory married, then became a priest, and finally bishop of Nyssa in Armenia in 372. He was involved in the controversies against Arianism, but was exiled, in part as a result of his inexperience and tactlessness. After the death of his brother Saint Basil the Great, he became prominent, especially at the first council of Constantinople. Of his many writings, his *Catechetical Discourse* is best-known. He also wrote a biography of his sister, Saint Macrina. His feast is celebrated on 9 March.

**Gregory the Great (the first), Pope Saint** (c.540-604) Born in Rome, he became prefect of the city. Then he entered a monastery, was ordained deacon and served as a papal legate in Constantinople. He became pope in 590; he reformed the papal administration, cared for the poor and wrote works on morals and doctrine. His influence on the Gregorian Sacramentary and Gregorian chant is uncertain. His feast is celebrated on 3 September.

**Grimald, Abbot** He was abbot of the monastery of Sankt Gallen in Switzerland from 841 to 872, and was also, for some time, archchancellor to King Louis the German. In his time, the monastery followed the Rule of Saint Benedict, but it had been founded in the Celtic tradition by the Irish hermit Saint Gall in 612.

**Heffernan, Enda** (1932-2001) A priest of the West American Province of the Capuchin Franciscan friars. A former Provincial Minister, he was active in retreat work.

**Hollings, Father Michael** ( -1997) An English Catholic priest who became widely known as a spiritual guide. He was a man who lived a very simple lifestyle and kept an open house for all comers, especially ethnic minorities, in his parish of Bayswater, London.

**Hume, George Basil** (1923-2000) English Benedictine monk, was abbot of Ampleforth in Yorkshire 1963-1976, became archbishop of Westminster in 1976, and then cardinal. Author of several books on spirituality.

**Ildefonsus, Saint** (? -667) Little is known of his early years, but he became bishop of Toledo in 657. He had a remarkable devotion to Mary, the mother of Jesus; it became a major feature of his preaching and left a mark on Spanish popular piety.

**Jerome, Saint** (340-420) Born at Strido, Croatia, he studied at Rome and was later baptised. He began to lead an ascetic life and was ordained priest against his will. He travelled widely before returning to Rome, becoming secretary to Pope Damasus and beginning the task of revising and re-translating the bible into Latin (the Vulgate), and of promoting the monastic life. An irascible man, given to extremes, he retired to Bethlehem where he continued writing on scripture until his death. His feast is celebrated on 30 September.

**John XXIII, Pope** (1881-1963) Born Angelo Roncalli at Sotto il Monte near Bergamo, Italy, after ordination he served in the papal diplomatic corps until becoming Patriarch of Venice. Elected pope in 1958, one year later he surprised the church by convoking a synod of the diocese of Rome, ordering the revision of the code of canon law, and the convocation of the Second Vatican Council, which began in 1962. Among his best-known writings are the encyclicals *Mater et Magistra* (1961) and *Pacem in Terris* (1963). He gave a powerful impetus to the promotion of Christian unity.

**John Chrysostom, Saint**. See Chrysostom, Saint John.

**John of Kronstadt** (1829-1908) A married priest of the Russian Orthodox church, John Sergeyev was chaplain to the naval base at Kronstadt near Saint Petersburg. Remembered as a 'praying priest' he drew large crowds from all parts of Russia to his preaching. His spiritual diary *My Life* *in Christ* has been published in English. He is regarded as a saint in parts of the Russian Orthodox church.

**John of the Cross, Saint** (about 1542-1591) Juan de Yepes y Alvarez was born at Fontiveros, Spain. He became a Carmelite in 1563 and was persuaded by Saint Teresa of Avila to undertake a reform of his Order, a task which caused him great suffering and even imprisonment. His writings, *The Ascent of Mount Carmel, The Spiritual Canticle, The Dark Night of the Soul* and his poems are classics of Christian spirituality. A doctor of the church, his feast is celebrated on 14 December.

**John Paul II, Pope** (1920- ) Born Karol Wojtyla at Wadowice, Poland, he studied clandestinely for the priesthood during the German occupation of his country during the Second World War. He became bishop in 1958, attended the Second Vatican Council and was elected pope in 1978, being the first non-Italian for four hundred years. He played a significant part in ending communist rule in central and eastern Europe. He has undertaken many pastoral visits to all continents and has written extensively on every aspect of church life.

**Johnston, William** Born in Belfast, Ireland, he joined the Jesuits and was ordained priest. He has spent many years in Japan where he became professor of religious studies at Sophia university in Tokyo. His contacts with Eastern mysticism have influenced his writing, and encouraged his involvement in dialogue with Buddhists. Among his best-known works are *The Inner Eye of Love, Silent Music* and *The Wounded Stag.* He is active in retreat work.

**Julian of Norwich** (1342-about 1420) An anchoress who lived at the church of Saints Julian and Edward at Norwich, England. Almost nothing is known of her, not even that her name was Julian; she may have been educated by local Benedictine nuns. She describes herself as 'a simple, unlearned creature' writing for 'the little and the simple.' She is best-known for her *Revelations*, an informal and conversational description of her mystical experiences, in which she speaks of God as mother. The influence of the Johannine writings is clear in her teaching on the divine indwelling, and of Saint Paul on her ideas on incorporation in Christ. The depth, joy and hopefulness of her writings show her to have been a person of real spiritual insight.

**Kentigern, Saint** (? - 603) A Scotsman also known as Mungo, meaning 'my darling', he became a missionary to the Britons in Strathclyde and became a bishop. Driven out by persecution, he continued working in Wales and the north-west of England before returning to Scotland. He is buried in Glasgow and his feast is celebrated on 14 January.

**Laud, William** (1573-1645) A priest of the Church of England, he became archbishop of Canterbury in 1633. His support for King Charles I brought the wrath of Parliament on him. He also alienated the propertied classes by enforcing laws regulating wages and prices, while his attempt to impose the Prayer Book on the Scots sparked off the English civil war. Impeached by Parliament, he was imprisoned in 1640 and then beheaded.

**Leo XIII, Pope** (1810-1903) Gioacchino Pecci was born at Carpineto, Italy. Becoming pope in 1878, he did much, especially through his encyclical letters, to restore the status of the Holy See. Among them, perhaps his best-known is *Rerum Novarum,* which dealt with social questions. He also contributed to the revival of scholastic theology.

**Leonine Sacramentary** The earliest surviving book of Roman Mass formularies and ordination prayers, it dates from the first quarter of the seventh century. Its compiler is unknown. It consists of a random collection of Mass texts, grouped by month. Although the contents are Roman in origin, they were not composed for use in Rome. Nor is there any clear connection, except perhaps in style, with Pope Saint Leo I (440-461) who collected Mass texts. It is also known as the Sacramentary of Verona, where the original text is kept in a single manuscript.

**Liguori, Alphonsus**. See Alphonsus Liguori, Saint.

**Liturgy**. The public worship of the church.

**Main, John** (1926-1982) Born in London, England, of Irish parents he was in turn a journalist, soldier, barrister and monk. He lectured in law at Trinity College, Dublin, before joining the Benedictines in 1959. Renowned for his spiritual writings, especially on meditation, he was the inspiration for the founding of the World Community for Christian Meditation which has about 1000 groups in some 40 countries. Among his best-known works are *Word into Silence, Moment of Christ* and *The Present Christ.*

**Makarios the Great, Saint** (c.300-c.390) Born in Upper Egypt, he began work as a camel-driver before becoming a monk and a priest in the desert of Skete (the Wadi al-Natrun). He was noted for his asceticism, shrewdness and gentleness. Many of his sayings are recorded in *The Sayings of the Desert Fathers*. His feast is celebrated in the Eastern churches on 19 January.

**Mark, the liturgy of Saint** The title given to the liturgical rites of the church of Alexandria, Egypt, and attributed to Saint Mark the evangelist. Before the Council of Chalcedon in 451, its language was Greek. After Chalcedon, Greek was used only by the Melchites, while the Copts and Ethiopians used Coptic and Ge'ez. It has not been used in Greek since the twelfth century. The earliest known fragments are a fourth century papyrus.

**Maronite Church, The** One of the Catholic Eastern churches, its members are found mainly in the Lebanon, Syria and, especially in recent years, in the United States. Claiming origin from Saint Maron (350-433), they follow the liturgy of Saint James in the Aramaic language. In full communion with Rome since the fifth Lateran Council (1512-1517) they are now almost completely Romanised.

**Maruta of Tikrit** (c.565-649) A monophysite brought up among Nestorians, Maruta was born near Balad, Iraq, joining the monastery of Niniveh in 605. He was made bishop of Tikrit, Iraq, with suffragans in Azerbaijan, Afghanistan and Iran. His writings, especially on the liturgy, had great influence on the Syrian Jacobites.

**Mozarabic liturgy** The origin of the term 'Mozarabic' is unclear. It describes the liturgy used in Iberia from the sixth to the eleventh centuries; also known as the Gothic liturgy since it arose during the Visigothic Kingdom in Spain. Its centre was Toledo, where it is still in use, and its principal architect was Saint Isidore of Seville. Of a common origin and almost identical construction to the Gallican liturgy.

**Newman, John Henry** (1801-1890) Born in London, England, Newman was ordained in the Church of England in 1824. He wrote a series of essays called *Tracts for the Times*, which gave rise to the Oxford Movement. He became a Catholic in 1845, and was made cardinal in 1879. From 1854-1858 he was rector of a projected Catholic University of Dublin, Ireland. Among his best-known writings are his autobiography, the *Apologia pro Vita Sua,* and the *Grammar of Assent*, an analysis of the nature of belief.

**Nicene Creed** A statement of the basic teachings of the Christian faith drawn up at the general council of Nicea in 325, and revised at the first council of Constantinople in 381. In 1014 it was adopted for use at Mass. It is this creed which is said at Mass on Sundays.

**Nicholas of Cusa** (1401-1464) German-born bishop of Brixen in the Tyrol, a philosopher, he is seen as being involved in the transition from scholasticism to modern philosophy. In his best-known work, *De docta Ignorantia* (Of learned Ignorance), he argued that God completely transcends human mental categories and dualisms, and is therefore above all knowledge, even the best of which is merely learned ignorance. In cosmology he broke with tradition by asserting that the universe is boundless.

**Niebuhr, Reinhold** (1892-1971) Born in the USA, he became a Lutheran minister. His best-known work is *Moral Man and Immoral Society*, which critiqued depersonalised industrial society and came to be known as Christian realism. He saw liberal democracy as the best available constraint on dictatorship.

**Obbard, Elizabeth Ruth** An American Carmelite nun, she has written *A Retreat with Thérèse of Lisieux: loving our way to holiness*.

**Ó Callanáin, Pádraig** A nineteenth-century Irish language poet who lived in Galway, Ireland.

**Orthodox** The name derives from the Greek *orthos*, true, and *doxa*, doctrine. The Orthodox churches are national churches of Eastern Europe, which, while possessing valid sacraments, have been separated from communion with the pope since the ninth century. Also called Byzantine, or Eastern, churches.

**Pachomius, Saint** (c.292-c.346) Born near Esneh, Egypt, he entered the army. On leaving it he became a Christian and a hermit but never became a priest. He gathered together hermits who followed the tradition of Saint Anthony of Egypt and is regarded as the founder of the monastic life. By the time of his death he had founded 9 communities of men and 2 of women, numbering in all about 3000 members. Saint Benedict of Norcia drew on Pachomius' rule when writing his own. His feast is kept on 9 May.

**Patrick, Saint** (about 385-461) Born in the west of Britain, he was brought up a Christian before being captured and taken to Ireland as a slave. He escaped, went to France and was ordained bishop about 432. Pope Celestine I sent him to bring the faith to the Christians of Ireland as successor to Palladius. Working through the chiefs, he achieved substantial success, founding his principal see at Armagh. Among the writings attributed to him, the *Confession* and the *Letter* *to Coroticus,* both warm human documents, are probably authentically his. His feast is celebrated on 17 March.

**Paul VI, Pope** (1897-1978) Born Giovanni Battista Montini near Brescia, Italy, he spent most of his life in the Vatican, except for five years from 1958 to 1963 as archbishop of Milan. Elected pope in 1963, his great work was the implementation of the decisions of the Second Vatican Council (1962-1965).

**Peter Canisius, Saint** (1521-1597) Born at Nijmegen, then in Germany, he joined the Jesuits and was ordained priest in 1546. He spent his life in the work of the Counter-Reformation, preaching, writing, teaching, founding schools, and arbitrating disputes across central Europe. Of his many writings, *The Catechism* is best remembered. His feast is celebrated on 21 December.

**Peter Damian, Saint** (1007-1072) Born at Ravenna, Italy, he became a hermit, but was later elected abbot of a monastery. By his writings, and later as cardinal, he did much to restore discipline among the clergy. His feast is celebrated on 21 February.

**Philoxenus** (c.450-523) Philoxenus was born in Tahal, Iran. He studied in Syria and became bishop there of Mabbugh (Hierapolis) in 485. His monophysitism has been described as more verbal than real; he opposed the council of Chalcedon, and was exiled but continued writing, being described as a creative and original thinker, a classical author in Syrian literature over a wide range of subjects.

**Pius IX, Pope** (1792-1878) Count Giovanni Mastai-Ferretti was born at Sinigaglia, Italy. Becoming pope in 1846, he attempted some reforms of the papal states, but without success. They were incorporated into the Kingdom of Italy in 1861 and Rome was included in 1870. He defined the doctrines of the Immaculate Conception of Mary in 1854 and papal infallibility in 1870 at the first Vatican Council (1869-1870).

**Pius XI, Pope** (1857-1939) Born Achille Ratti near Milan, Italy, he became pope in 1922. He normalised the relationship between the Holy See and Italy by the Lateran Treaty of 1929, was a vigorous promoter of missionary work, especially of the need for a local clergy, and opposed totalitarianism, writing encyclical letters against fascism *(Non abbiamo bisogno)*, nazism *(Mit brennender Sorge)* and communism *(Divini Redemptoris)*.

**Pius XII, Pope** (1876-1958) Eugenio Pacelli was born in Rome. After ordination he joined the Vatican diplomatic corps, serving mainly in Germany, before becoming secretary of state, and then pope in March 1939. Several of his encyclical letters helped prepare the way for later developments at Vatican II.

**Pontifical** A book of liturgical texts containing the rites of ordinations and consecrations reserved to a bishop. The first Roman pontifical was published in 1485.

**Powell, John** An American priest of the Society of Jesus, he writes widely on spirituality, combining insights from psychology.

**Processional** A liturgical book containing the order to be followed in a procession; in medieval times, a book with information on a local church.

**Prosper of Aquitaine, Saint** (c.400-c.463) Prosper, a layman, was born in Gascony, France. He spent his life in Provence. An enthusiastic follower of Saint Augustine, his teaching on free will and grace was opposed by some of the French bishops. Pope Celestine, at Prosper's urging, criticised the bishops for their opposition. His feast is celebrated by the Augustinians on 25 June.

**Psalter** The Old Testament collection of 150 psalms, or a book containing the same, arranged for the recitation of the Divine Office individually or in common.

**Redemptorists** The Congregation of the Most Holy Redeemer (C.Ss.R.), a Catholic religious congregation founded by Saint Alphonsus Liguori in 1732. Its members in Ireland have published *Come, Lord Jesus*: *Redemptorist Mission and Novena Book*, Redemptorist Publications, Dublin, no date.

**Rice, Blessed Edmund Ignatius** (1762-1844) Born in Callan, Kilkenny, Ireland, into a wealthy family, Edmund married in 1785. However, his wife died just 4 years later and their only child was handicapped. From his earliest years he had cared for poor children, feeding and teaching them. In 1802 he began his first school; other men joined him and the Congregation of Christian Brothers and later Presentation Brothers, came into being. Today, they have schools of all kinds on five continents. He was declared Blessed in 1996.

**Ritual** A book containing the texts of liturgical rites.

**Robert of Jumièges** (? -1055) Robert was born in Normandy, France. Entering the Benedictines, he became abbot of Jumièges in 1037. He was chosen by his friend King Edward the Confessor to be bishop of London in 1044, and transferred to Canterbury in 1051. After only one year, he was deposed through political infighting and retired to Jumièges where he directed the preparation of a Missal in the Anglo-Saxon style bearing his name.

**Robinson, Wendy** An English mother of three children, she wrote *Exploring Silence* among other works.

**Rolheiser, Ronald** A Canadian priest, a member of the Oblates of Mary Immaculate, he writes frequently on spiritual matters in books and newspapers, and is engaged in retreat work.

**Rolle, Richard** (about 1300-1349) Born Richard Rolle de Hampole in north Yorkshire, England, he seems to have attended Oxford University but not to have graduated. He never received holy orders, but lived an eremetical life. His early writings were often quarrelsome and harshly critical of others but, in later years, he matured somewhat and his best works were those where he wrote simply for ordinary people, in particular his poems and songs of the love of God.

**Roman** Of the Roman Catholic church.

**Sacramentary** A book containing the rites of the sacraments, including the rite of celebrating Mass. The term is sometimes used more narrowly as a synonym for a Missal. In the Western tradition, some the best-known are the Celtic, Franciscan, Gallican, Gelasian, Gregorian, Leonine, Milanese and Mozarabic.

**Sarum** The word derives from Sarisburia, the Latin name for Salisbury, England, one of the principal English episcopal sees. Beginning with missionaries sent to England by Pope Saint Gregory I in 596 under Saint Augustine of Canterbury, a musical tradition developed which, with Gallican and Norman French influences after 1066, lasted until the Reformation. It was revived by Anglicans scholars in the nineteenth century. Other liturgical texts, such as the Primer, claim origin from Salisbury.

**Scottish Psalter** The first version of the Scottish Psalter, or book of psalms, influenced by that of Geneva, was produced in 1564 by Protestant groups who had left Britain because of religious persecution. There were several later editions, of which that of 1650 exchanged artistic vitality for practical usefulness, and reduced the metrical patterns of earlier editions to the monotony of the English common metre.

**Shaw, Gilbert** (1886-1967) Born in Dublin, Ireland, he began his career as a barrister, married and had a family, and then became a clergyman in the Church of England. His *Pilgrim's Book of Prayers* was first published in 1945. Active in retreat work, he was warden of the Sisters of the Love of God in Oxford from 1964 until his death.

**Siemens, Werner von** (1816-1892) A German electrical engineer who discovered the dynamo principle in 1867. He founded a highly successful company which built trams and hydro-electric stations, and operated intercontinental telephone systems.

**Silouan of Mount Athos, Saint** (1866-1938) Born in a Russian village, Silouan entered the Russian monastery on Mount Athos, Greece, in 1892, and remained there for the rest of his life. Never ordained, he was a *starets*, a spiritual adviser, who particularly urged forgiveness of one another. His writings were published after his death by his disciple, Archimandrite Sophrony under the titles *The Monk of Mount Athos* and *Wisdom from Mount Athos*.

**Society of Saint Francis** A religious order of Anglican Franciscans, founded in England, now widespread in the English-speaking world.

**Solzhenitsyn, Alexander Isayevich** (1918- ) A writer and member of the Russian Orthodox church, he was imprisoned from 1945 to 1957 for criticism of Stalin. His writings, especially *The Gulag Archipelago*, were critical of the Soviet system. He was expelled from the Soviet Union in 1974 and went to live in the USA where he became a citizen. He was awarded the Nobel prize for literature in 1970.

**Soubirous, Saint Marie Bernarde (Bernadette)** (1844-1879) Born in poverty and ill-health at Lourdes, France, she was favoured with the apparitions there of our Lady of the Immaculate Conception in 1858. Suffering much as a result, in 1866 she joined the Sisters of Notre Dame at Nevers where she spent the rest of her life. Her feast is celebrated on 16 April.

**Stein, Saint Edith** (1891-1942) Born into a Jewish family in Germany, she was an atheist for some time. Drawn to the Catholic faith through the writings of Saint Teresa of Avila, she became a Carmelite nun with the name of Sister Teresa

Benedicta of the Cross. She was arrested by German occupation forces in the Netherlands, taken to Auschwitz concentration camp, and killed. In 1988 Pope John Paul II canonised her amid controversy and declared her co-patroness of Europe. Her feast is kept on 9 August.

**Sulivan, Jean** (1913-1980) The pseudonym of a French diocesan priest whose spiritual journal has been published in English under the title *Morning Light*. He has also written *The Sea Remains* and *Eternity my Beloved*. He was killed in a road accident.

**Syrian liturgy** Originally the rite of the church of Antioch, Syria, dating from the fourth century, it was written in Greek; in later centuries Syriac was used, and Arabic in modern times. The rite is used today by Jacobites (Monophysites) and Catholics in Syria and Lebanon. One of its features is the Liturgy of Saint James, which has sixty-four Eucharistic prayers.

**Talmud, The** A collection of teachings of Jewish rabbis, consisting of the Mishna and a commentary on it, the Gemara, in two editions, in the fourth and fifth centuries A.D. From the Aramaic for *teaching*.

**Tauler, John** (1304-1361) Probably born in Strasbourg, France, he joined the Dominicans and studied in Cologne, where he met and was influenced by Blessed Henry Suso and Meister Eckhart. Many of his sermons survive; they focus especially on the nature and attributes of God.

**Teresa of Ávila, Saint** (1515-1582) Born in Spain, she joined the Carmelites in her home town, where she led a relaxed and comfortable life. However, in 1562 she led a reform movement based on a return to the authentic tradition of Carmel. Supported by Saint Peter of Alcántara and working with Saint John of the Cross, she set up sixteen houses of the reform, despite ill-health, intense opposition and a lack of resources. Her writings, especially her *Life, The Interior Castle* and *The Way of Perfection* are among the great classics of Christian spirituality. They combine spiritual insight, humour, kindness and hard-headed realism. She was declared a doctor of the church in 1970 by Pope Paul VI and her feast is celebrated on 15 October.

**Teresa of Calcutta, Mother** (1910-1997) Born Agnes Gonxha Bojaxhiu in Skopje, Macedonia and educated in Ireland, she joined the Loreto Sisters and taught in their schools in India. Her 'second vocation', to serve 'the poorest of the poor' led her to live among, and work with, destitute people in Calcutta. In 1948 she founded the Missionaries of Charity, now a worldwide congregation of sisters, engaging in similar work. She was awarded the Nobel Peace prize in 1979.

**Thomas Aquinas, Saint** (1225-1274) Born in Aquino, Italy, he studied at Monte Cassino and Paris, and at Cologne under Saint Albert the Great. A Dominican friar, he was perhaps the greatest philosopher and theologian of the church, and has left a large body of writings. His principal works are the *Summa contra Gentiles* and the *Summa Theologica;* he has also left some religious poems, especially the Office for *Corpus Christi.*

**Turgenyev, Ivan Sergeyevich** (1818-1883) Russian novelist and playwright, noted for realism and pessimism.

**Vatican II**. The Second Vatican Council, called by Pope John XXIII, was held in Rome 1962-65, to promote renewal of the Roman Catholic Church and unity with the other Christian churches.

**Voillaume, René** Was for a time the superior of the Little Brothers of Jesus founded by Charles de Foucauld. Among his writings are *Seeds of the Desert.*

**Ware, Kallistos** A fellow of Pembroke College, Oxford, and a bishop of the Orthodox church, he has written on spirituality. Among his writings are *The Power of the Name,* a study of the Jesus prayer.

**Way of a Pilgrim, The** An anonymous work of spirituality, written in Russia, probably between 1853 and 1861. The second part, *The Pilgrim continues his Way*, was probably written by another author.

**Weimarischer Gesangbuch** A Lutheran hymnal produced at Weimar, Germany, in 1873.

**Wesley, John** (1703-1791) Born at Epworth, Lincolnshire, England, he went to Oxford with his brother Charles. They were so methodical in their religious observances that they were nicknamed Methodists. Ordained in the Church of England, he went to Georgia, USA, as a missionary. He returned to England in 1738 and experienced a conversion which changed him from High Anglican to evangelical. When he was prohibited from preaching in Anglican churches, he brought the gospel to the people, travelling round the country on horseback for some fifty years, preaching in the open air. His sermons became the doctrinal basis of Methodism.

**Young Christian Workers** A movement, founded by Joseph Cardijn, a Belgian priest, later cardinal, which sought to strengthen the faith of the young when they entered modern industrial urbanised society. Using the slogan 'See, judge, act' they were encouraged to observe and assess their situation in the light of the Christian faith, and to become active both in mutual support and spreading the faith. The movement is present in about 120 countries.

# Index of Documents
# of the Second Vatican Council
# (Vatican II, 1962-1965)

**Ad Gentes:** the decree on the church's missionary activity.

**Apostolicam Actuositatem:** the decree on the apostolate of laypeople.

**Christus Dominus:** the decree on the pastoral office of bishops.

**Dei Verbum:** the dogmatic constitution on divine revelation.

**Dignitatis Humanae:** the declaration on religious liberty.

**Gaudium et Spes:** the pastoral constitution on the church in the modern world.

**Gravissimum Educationis:** the declaration on Christian education.

**Inter Mirifica:** the decree on the instruments of social communication.

**Lumen Gentium:** the dogmatic constitution on the church.

**Nostra Aetate:** the declaration on the church's relationship with non-Christian religions.

**Optatam Totius:** the decree on the training of priests.

**Orientalium Ecclesiarum:** the decree on the Catholic eastern churches.

**Perfectae Caritatis:** the decree on the renewal and adaptation of the religious life.

**Presbyterorum Ordinis:** the decree on the life and ministry of priests.

**Sacrosanctum Concilium:** the constitution on the liturgy.

**Unitatis Redintegratio:** the decree on ecumenism.

# Index of Psalms

| Psalm | Page |
|---|---|
| 4 | 48 |
| 15 | 53 |
| 22 | 106 |
| 29 | 62 |
| 31 | 80 |
| 33:2-9 | 78 |
| 33:10-15 | 86 |
| 70 | 60 |
| 76 | 16 |
| 85 | 44 |
| 97 | 24 |
| 111 | 90 |
| 115 | 14 |
| 118:9-16 | 36 |
| 141 | 50 |
| 145 | 28 |

# Index of Biblical Canticles

**Old Testament Canticles**                                       **Page**
1 Chronicles 16:23-25, 27                                          82
1 Chronicles 29:10-13                                              67
Nehemiah 8:6; Jeremiah 33:11; Ezekiel 3:12                         110
Tobit 3:11-12; 8:5; 11:14                                          84
Tobit 13:1, 4-6                                                    100
Isaiah 33:13, 15-16                                                72
Isaiah 53:4, 5, 7, 8, 10, 12                                       86
Daniel 3:52-59                                                     79

**New Testament Canticles**
Ephesians 2:4-6,8,10                                               108
Ephesians 3:14-21                                                  44
Colossians 1:9-14                                                  98
Colossians 1:12-20                                                 10
Revelation 4:11; 5:9, 10, 12                                       120
Revelation 11:15; 19:1-2; 7:12                                     116

# Common Prayers

**The Sign of the Cross**
In the name of the Father, and of the Son, and of the Holy Spirit. Amen.

**Our Father**
Our Father, who art in heaven,
 hallowed be thy name;
thy Kingdom come;
 thy will be done on earth as it is in heaven.
Give us this day our daily bread;
and forgive us our trespasses
 as we forgive those who trespass against us;
and lead us not into temptation,
 but deliver us from evil. Amen.

**Hail, Mary**
Hail, Mary, full of grace, the Lord is with you!
Blessed are you among women,
 and blessed is the fruit of your womb, Jesus.
Holy Mary, Mother of God, pray for us sinners
 now and at the hour of our death. Amen.

**Glory**
Glory be to the Father,
and to the Son,
and to the Holy Spirit,
as it was in the beginning,
is now, and ever shall be,
world without end. Amen.

**An act of sorrow**
My God, I thank you for loving me.
I am sorry for all my sins,
for not loving others and for not loving you.
Help me to live like Jesus lived,
and not sin again. Amen.

**The Apostles' Creed**
I believe in God, the Father almighty, creator of heaven and earth.

I believe in Jesus Christ, his only Son, our Lord.
He was conceived by the power of the Holy Spirit
and born of the Virgin Mary.
He suffered under Pontius Pilate,
was crucified, died, and was buried.
He descended to the dead.
On the third day he rose again.
He ascended into heaven,
and is seated at the right hand of the Father.
He will come again to judge the living and the dead.

I believe in the Holy Spirit,
the holy catholic church,
the communion of saints,
the forgiveness of sins,
the resurrection of the body,
and the life everlasting. Amen.

**The Nicene Creed**

We believe in one God,
the Father, the Almighty,
maker of heaven and earth,
of all that is, seen and unseen.

We believe in one Lord, Jesus Christ,
the only Son of God,
eternally begotten of the Father,
God from God, Light from Light,
true God from true God,
begotten, not made, of one Being with the Father.
Through him all things were made.
For us and for our salvation
he came down from heaven:
by the power of the Holy Spirit
he became incarnate from the Virgin Mary,
and was made man.

For our sake he was crucified under Pontius Pilate;
he suffered death and was buried.
On the third day he rose again
in accordance with the Scriptures;
he ascended into heaven
and is seated at the right hand of the Father.
He will come again in glory to judge the living and the dead,
and his Kingdom will have no end.

We believe in the Holy Spirit, the Lord, the giver of life,
who proceeds from the Father and the Son.
With the Father and the Son he is worshipped and glorified.
He has spoken through the Prophets.
We believe in one holy catholic and apostolic church
We acknowledge one baptism for the forgiveness of sins.
We look for the resurrection of the dead,
and the life of the world to come. Amen.